Working in accounting and finance

Tutorial

Michael Fardon

AAT WISE GUIDES – for convenient exam revision

This handy pocket-sized guide provides the **perfect study and revision resource** for the AAT Level 2 Certificate in Accounting.

available for:
Bookkeeping 1
Bookkeeping 2
Working in Accounting and Finance
Introduction to Costing

Visit www.osbornebooks.co.uk for further information and to place your order.

© Michael Fardon, 2013. Reprinted 2014 (twice).

Published by Osborne Books Limited
Unit 1B Everoak Estate
Bromyard Road, Worcester WR2 5HP
Tel 01905 748071
Email books@osbornebooks.co.uk
Website www.osbornebooks.co.uk

Design by Laura Ingham

Printed by CPI Group (UK) Limited, Croydon, CR0 4YY,
an environmentally friendly, acid-free paper from managed forests.

British Library Cataloguing in Publication Data
A catalogue record for this book is available from the British Library

ISBN 978 1909173 071

Contents

Acknowledgements

The publisher wishes to thank the following for their help with the reading and production of the book: Maz Loton and Cathy Turner. Thanks are also due to Roger Petheram for technical advice with the earlier (2010) version of this book and to Alison Aplin for her technical reading and Laura Ingham for her designs for this series.

The publisher is indebted to the Association of Accounting Technicians for its help and advice to our authors and editors during the preparation of this text.

Author

Michael Fardon has extensive teaching experience of a wide range of banking, business and accountancy courses at Worcester College of Technology. He now specialises in writing business and financial texts and is General Editor at Osborne Books. He is also an educational consultant and has worked extensively in the areas of vocational business curriculum development.

Introduction

what this book covers

This book has been written specifically to cover the Unit 'Work Effectively in Accounting and Finance' which is mandatory for the revised (2013) AAT Level 2 Certificate in Accounting.

The book contains a clear text with illustrative examples and case studies, chapter summaries and key terms to help with revision. Each chapter has a wide range of student activities, many based on the style of the AAT assessment.

A major new feature in this text is a chapter on professional ethics and sustainability, two areas which are significant issues affecting the way in which a modern organisation operates.

Osborne Workbooks

Osborne Workbooks contain practice material which helps students achieve success in their assessments. *Working in Accounting and Finance Workbook* contains a number of paper-based 'fill in' practice exams in the style of the computer-based assessment. Please visit www.osbornebooks.co.uk for further details and access to our online shop.

1 Accounting and finance in the workplace

this chapter covers...

This chapter is an introduction to the role played by the accounting function in the workplace; it shows how accounting 'works' in an organisation such as a business. It describes the various areas in which accounting and finance staff are likely to work and the way in which the size of the organisation will affect job roles and working relationships.

The chapter explains the following:

- *the difference between bookkeeping and accounting – bookkeeping involves the keeping of financial records and accounting involves the processing and reporting of this financial information*

- *accounting has a number of important roles within a business, including recording financial information, financial reporting, forecasting, planning and managing*

- *financial accounting deals with external reporting of past events, whereas management accounting deals with internal financial forecasting and planning*

- *basic accounting carried out by bookkeepers and accounts assistants involves a wide variety of areas – sales order processing, purchasing, cashiering, payroll, costing and stock control*

- *in larger organisations the basic accounting staff report to financial and management accounting managers and auditors along defined reporting lines*

- *an effective working environment will have efficient reporting lines*

ACCOUNTING AND FINANCE FUNCTIONS

accounting and finance

The terms 'accounting' and 'finance' are sometimes used loosely to relate to 'dealing with money', but it is important to be able to distinguish between the two and identify the functions they fulfil in an organisation.

It is easier to start with finance because it has a more restricted meaning:

Finance involves providing and managing funds and resources for an organisation such as a business.

If you work in a 'finance' company you are likely to lend money or provide products such as hire purchase. If you work in a finance department you are likely to be involved in managing money and other resources.

Accounting, on the other hand, involves rather more than this:

Accounting is a system for recording, analysing and reporting financial transactions and the financial status of a business.

Accounting is based on finance, but it takes things further, analysing and reporting financial data.

accounting – the oldest profession in the world?

Accounting has sometimes been described as one of the oldest professions in the world. The word **accounting** involves a number of concepts which have been in use since the Egyptian Pharoahs built the pyramids:

■ keeping financial records – 'accounts' – of money spent and money received in relation to a project or a business

■ using this information to 'account' to people who have interest in the project or business, for example the owners or the people providing the money – giving estimates of income, spending (expenses), making a profit or a loss, calculating money owed and money due

a note on keeping records – bookkeeping

The task of keeping records of financial transactions such as income and expenses forms the 'nuts and bolts' of accounting. Traditionally known as bookkeeping, it developed over six hundred years ago in Italy into a double-entry system which involved every transaction being recorded in two separate 'accounts'. **Bookkeeping**, therefore, is the process of keeping financial records; **accounting**, on the other hand, takes the process further, analysing and reporting this information to business owners and other people who are interested in the business, the stakeholders. These 'stakeholders' include the public, the government, lenders, customers and suppliers.

present-day functions of accounting

In order to act in the interests of the business and its stakeholders, accounting staff have to carry out a wide range of functions, including:

- **recording and reporting**

  recording data and preparing financial reports about what has happened in the past – sales figures, income statements, tax calculations, VAT returns

- **forecasting**

  preparing financial forecasts and budgets – these are estimates of what is expected to happen in the future

- **monitoring and control**

  comparing the figures in forecasts and budgets with what actually happens and then taking corrective action if the figures are off target

- **external auditing**

  checking by external and independent accountants that the recording of financial transactions within the organisation is accurate and in accordance with rules laid down by external regulatory bodies

- **internal auditing**

  checking by the organisation's own staff that the recording of financial transactions is accurate and in accordance with internal rules

In short, accounting is concerned with

- **recording** financial data
- **reporting** financial data
- **planning** for the organisation's future – setting objectives and targets
- **managing** the organisation – taking action if the targets are not met

financial and management accounting

Accounting is traditionally divided into two types – financial accounting and management accounting:

- **financial accounting** is involved with financial transactions that have already happened and with the preparation and interpretation of financial statements for the benefit of managers, the owners and in some cases the external stakeholders of an organisation

- **management accounting** deals with all aspects of providing financial data to management (eg future income and costs) so that planning can take place and decisions made, eg reducing or increasing selling prices or switching resources from one product or service to another

ACCOUNTING ROLES

In this section we look at the different roles carried out by people working in accounting jobs. It must be appreciated that there are many different types of organisation that carry out accounting processes: some large, many small, some state-owned or controlled and many privately owned.

Whatever the organisation, the accounting function must still take place. Generally speaking the larger the organisation, the greater the need for control and accountability to outside stakeholders. In a smaller business – a sole trader local taxi service, for example – the accounting records are far less complex and the owner only accountable to himself/herself and to the tax authorities.

basic accounting roles

Anyone can keep the 'books' of a business; the important point is that they must be kept accurately – by the owner, or by a full or part-time bookkeeper or accounts assistant employed for the purpose. Bookkeepers do not have to be qualified, although it is better if they are. The basic accounting roles can be performed by someone coming in for a day a week to write up the books of a small business, or by hundreds of accounting staff employed by the accounts departments of larger companies. The books may be hand-written, or more often than not, computerised.

In a small business the bookkeeper or accounts assistant is likely to carry out a wide variety of tasks (see diagram on the next page), for example:

- **sales order processing**: taking sales orders, producing invoices, monitoring receipts – all the jobs connected with the sales ledger
- **purchasing**: sending out orders, checking the incoming documentation, making payments – all the jobs connected with the purchases ledger
- **cashiering** – recording incoming and outgoing payments and dealing with cash held in the business – all the jobs connected with the cash book or the petty cash book
- **payroll** – maintaining payroll records, calculating the payroll and processing payroll payments

Other specialist accounting jobs include:

- **costing** – working out the figures for the cost of products and services and preparing reports for management
- **inventory control** – monitoring and re-ordering inventory

In a larger business, because of the volume of transactions, these jobs are likely to be departmentalised; employees are likely to remain in one specialist accounting area and gain expertise there.

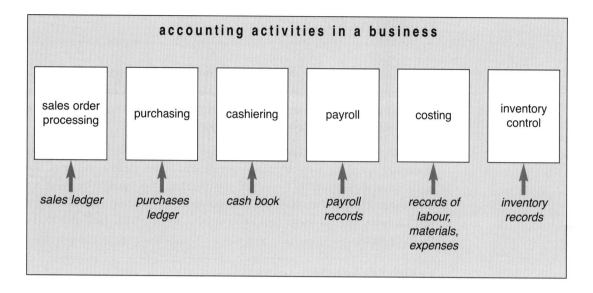

accountants in the organisation

The role of the **accountant** – who should be professionally qualified – is to check, summarise, present, analyse and interpret the accounts for the benefit of the owner/owners and other interested parties. In larger organisations accountants form the next level up from the accounts assistants. They may be:

■ line managers, supervising the work of the accounts assistants

■ senior managers, taking responsibility for specific functional areas

There are three main types of specialist accountant:

■ **financial accountants**, who deal with internal and external reporting

■ **management accountants**, who deal with reporting and budgeting

■ **auditors**, who check that the accounting procedures have been carried out correctly

financial accountant

The function of the **financial accountant** is very much concerned with financial transactions, and with using the information produced by the bookkeeper or accounts assistant. The financial accountant extracts information from the accounting records in order to provide a method of control, for example, over customers who buy on credit, over suppliers, cash and bank balances.

The role of a financial accountant also involves the periodic analysis and reporting of financial data so that financial statements – such as the statement of profit or loss and the statement of financial position – can be prepared for internal use and also for external use.

management accountant

The **management accountant** obtains information about costs – eg the cost of labour, materials, expenses (overheads) – and interprets the data and prepares reports and budgets for the owners or managers of the business. In particular, the management accountant is concerned with financial decision-making, planning and control of the business.

auditors

Auditors are accountants whose role is to check that accounting procedures have been followed correctly. There are two types of auditors: external auditors and internal auditors.

External auditors are independent of the business whose accounts are being audited. They are normally members of firms of accountants. The most common type of audit conducted by external auditors is the audit of larger limited companies required by law. In this situation, the auditors are reporting to the shareholders of a company, stating that the legal requirements laid down in the Companies Acts have been complied with, and that the accounts represent a 'true and fair view' of the state of the business.

Internal auditors are employed or contracted by the business which they audit. Their duties are concerned with the internal check and control procedures of the business, for example monitoring the procedures for the control of cash, and the authorisation of purchases. The nature of their work requires that they should have a degree of independence within the company.

HOW ACCOUNTING SUPPORTS THE ORGANISATION

The accounting function in an organisation fulfils an important support role to the other functions in the organisation. The accounting function can provide the other departments with information about the financial implications of their activities. For example:

- the sales ledger section can keep sales representatives updated with the credit status of their customers, highlighting any slow payers
- the purchases ledger section can advise the Administration Department of how much is owed to suppliers for purchases and overhead expenses
- the payroll section can advise the Human Resources Department about payroll costs, for example how much overtime was paid last month
- the costing section can advise the Production Department on the direct costs of production (eg materials) and also the overhead costs of production
- the cashier handles and records the cash sales for the Sales Department

This support of the organisation by the accounting functions is shown below:

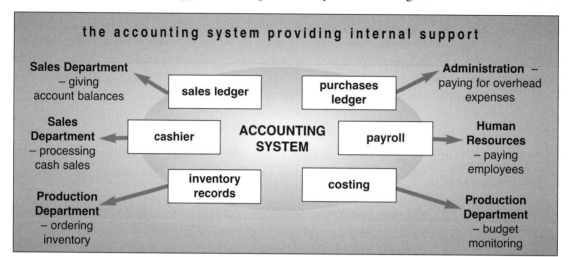

the features of effective information

In order for information to be effective it must be:

- **complete** – there is no point in giving information if something is missing
- **accurate** – incorrect information can lead to mistakes and confusion
- **timely** – the information must be given promptly and be up-to-date
- **fit for purpose** – it must be relevant and usable by the recipient

Any shortcomings in the information – eg incorrect wages paid, incorrect stock delivered or failure to pay bills and suppliers – will detract from the efficiency and reputation of the organisation.

REPORTING LINES

the structure of the business

The diagram on the next page is based on the accounting roles in a large company and illustrates the structure of the business. The boxes with the dark grey background all represent accounting roles. You will see that the structure is set out in a series of layers of authority and responsibility. This type of structure is known as a 'hierarchy': the lowest level is made up of the bookkeepers and accounts assistants, and as you move up the structure, the people involved gain both power and responsibility.

reporting lines between levels

You will also see that the arrows represent 'up and down' **reporting lines** within the organisation. A reporting line simply means that the people lower

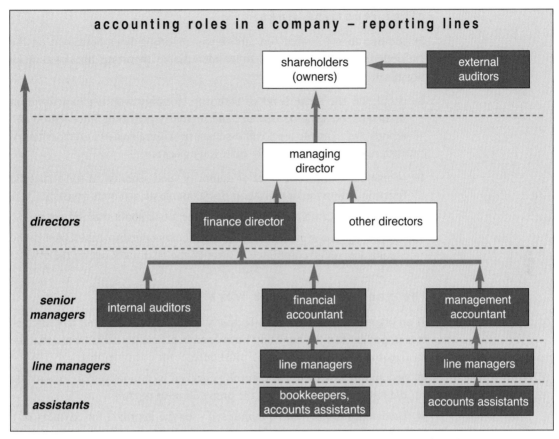

accounting roles in a company – reporting lines

Note: the boxes with a dark grey background represent the people carrying out an accounting role.

down in the structure always report to the next layer up: accounts assistants report to line managers, who in turn report to the senior managers, who in turn report to the directors of the company. This word 'report' has various meanings. For example, a lower level is able to pass on to a higher level:

■ specific information that is required or has been requested

■ regular reports that are needed

■ day-to-day work for approval and authorisation

■ complaints about the work, work conditions or colleagues

■ suggestions about how to improve the way the work is organised

It follows that the higher level in the company has the authority to:

■ request information

■ commission reports

■ approve and authorise work carried out at the lower level

■ deal with complaints and resolve the issue (or pass it to the next level up)

■ organise discussions about the way the work is organised

other reporting lines

In addition to the formal 'up and down' reporting lines described on the previous two pages there are other identifiable reporting lines within an organisation. These include:

■ people **on the same level** of authority, possibly working in a different section of the same department and regularly providing information and reports, for example a payroll assistant providing details to the cashier of cash required for the weekly cash wage packets

■ people **on a different level** of authority and reported to for a specific function within the organisation, for example an accounts assistant

  - reporting to a training manager to have a talk about training needs

  - reporting as a representative of the accounts department elected to the company social committee to arrange the next night out on the town

the need for effective working

If an organisation is to work effectively, smoothly and without any hitches, it is important that the reporting lines operate efficiently. This means that the management of the organisation must ensure, for example, that:

■ accounting tasks must be carefully checked by a more senior person – eg the issue of a sales invoice, the preparation of payroll

■ accounting tasks must be authorised – eg the approval for payment of a purchase invoice, processing of payroll

■ problems with any accounting system should be reported to a higher authority

■ requests for information or a report should be clear and a realistic timescale indicated

The same holds true for reporting lines which involve people on the same level or people such as training managers.

It is critical that all employees should know:

■ the identity and status of the people to whom they should report

■ what they have to report

If this is not made clear to employees there will be communication problems with the reporting lines, errors are likely to be made and complaints will be received. This could result in money losses and damage to the reputation of the organisation. As mentioned earlier, in a small business the accounting tasks are likely to be carried out by a limited number of people. In this case there will not be many reporting lines but the need for efficiency by the few people involved will become all the more important.

Chapter Summary

■ **Finance** involves providing and managing funds and resources for an organisation such as a business, whereas **accounting** is a system for recording, analysing and reporting financial transactions and the financial position of a business.

■ **Accounting** has a number of basic roles within a business, including the recording of financial information, financial reporting, forecasting, planning and managing.

■ **Financial accounting** deals with the reporting of past financial transactions and their presentation in financial statements both for internal and external use.

■ **Management accounting** provides past and projected financial data to managers so that forward planning can take place in the form of budgets, and decisions made about the use of resources.

■ **Bookkeepers** and **accounts assistants** deal with the basic financial records of an organisation in a number of defined areas:
  - sales order processing
  - purchasing
  - cashiering
  - payroll
  - costing
  - inventory control

■ **Accountants** are the qualified managers of the accounting function. They may be line managers (supervisors) or more senior managers and are likely to have a specific area of responsibility.

■ **Auditors** are accountants whose role it is to check that accounting procedures have been followed correctly and that no shady practices are taking place. Internal auditors are employees of the organisation and look over its accounting systems; external auditors are independent outsiders who are contracted by the shareholders of larger companies to validate the accounts.

■ The accounting functions within an organisation provide support to other departments and information about the financial implications of their activities.

■ A **reporting line** is the direct relationship between a manager and the people who work under him/her. It involves the passing of information, suggestions and complaints. Well-developed reporting lines are essential in any well-run organisation, especially the larger organisations.

Key Terms	finance	providing and managing funds and other resources for an organisation
	bookkeeping	recording financial transactions
	accounting	recording, analysing and reporting financial information
	financial accounting	analysis and reporting of past financial transactions in financial statements
	management accounting	providing past and projected financial information for managers to help with planning, decision making and control
	stakeholder	a person or organisation that has an interest in the financial performance of a business
	internal auditing	internal checking of the financial records by an employee of the organisation
	external auditing	external checking of the financial records by independent accountants
	reporting line	the line of communication between different levels within an organisation

Activities

1.1 Which one of the following jobs can best be described as a job in 'finance'?

(a) bank lending officer

(b) management accountant

(c) bookkeeper

1.2 Which one of the following jobs can best be described as a job in 'accounting'?

(a) mortgage lender

(b) auditor

(c) bookkeeper

1.3   A financial accountant is a person who

(a)   prepares an income statement for the last financial year

(b)   sets budgets for the next financial year

(c)   checks the accounts of a business

Which one of these options is correct?

1.4   A management accountant is a person who

(a)   prepares an income statement for the last financial year

(b)   checks the accounts of a business

(c)   sets budgets for the next financial year

Which one of these options is correct?

1.5   Explain the difference between an internal auditor and an external auditor.

1.6   The diagram below shows the organisational structure of an accounts department in a small business which buys and sells goods on credit.

Study the diagram and answer the questions that follow.

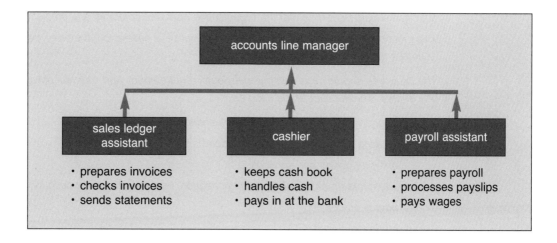

(a)   Identify the three reporting lines in the diagram.

(b)   Which assistant would the line manager ask if she wanted a report on customers who were bad payers?

(c)   If the payroll assistant wanted to complain that there were not the right number of £20 notes available for the wage packets, to whom would he complain

(1)   in the first place?

(2)   in the second place, if there was still a problem?

(d)   What other 'assistant level' accounting roles might also feature in this diagram, which shows a business that buys and sells goods on credit?

2 Efficiency and regulation in the workplace

this chapter covers...

This chapter examines the way in which the accounting and finance function of a business should be run so that the organisation operates smoothly and efficiently.

This means that the business should remain solvent – ie have enough money with which to pay its debts as they become due.

The business should also comply with legal requirements and internal policies and procedures. These cover areas such as:

- *accounting and finance: regulations relating to*
  - *keeping the accounts and other records*
  - *ordering goods and services*
  - *payments (cash handling, writing cheques, operating the bank account)*
  - *payroll processing*
  - *storing documents*

- *a code of conduct for the office: use of the internet, employee conduct*

- *health and safety: maintaining a safe and hazard-free working environment*

- *confidentiality: dealing with customer details, processing employee payroll*

- *'green' policies*

- *working hours: the maximum hours an employee should work*

Some of these procedures are based on regulations set down in law, and this will be highlighted where appropriate in the chapter, although it should be stressed that knowledge of individual laws is not required, just the appreciation that there are legal obligations with which the organisation must comply.

A SMOOTH RUNNING ORGANISATION

the need for efficiency

The last chapter explained how the accounting and finance functions of an organisation support the other departments by providing information. It is critical that this information is:

■ **complete** – all the information needed is provided

■ **accurate** – the information must be 100% correct

■ **on time** – the information should be provided within the given timescale

If all these three conditions listed above are fulfilled by the staff working in accounting and finance roles, it contributes to the **efficiency** of the organisation – its smooth running and its profitability.

'Efficiency' can be described as 'achieving the right result with the minimum of wasted time, effort or expense.' Efficiency is an important objective for any organisation.

achieving efficiency in the workplace

There are various ways in which efficiency in the workplace can be maintained and improved:

■ by the **individual employee**:
  - treating other employees and management with respect
  - taking pride in the tasks performed and making sure that the accounting procedures are fully understood
  - being familiar with and updating when necessary the various accounting tasks in written form (a 'procedures manual') for the benefit of others who are training on the job
  - pursuing CPD 'Continuing Professional Development' - ie training and qualifications for the job (see Chapter 8)

■ by the **employer**:
  - treating the employees with respect and encouraging motivation
  - ensuring that accounting procedures are followed properly
  - arranging appropriate training (as part of CPD) so that each employee's job is done properly and expertly
  - ensuring that there is sufficient staff to cover the accounting tasks
  - making sure the staff do not work very long hours
  - ensuring that the staff are paid an acceptable wage, which must be at least the Minimum Wage (see page 28)

the need for solvency

'**Solvency' means being able to pay your debts when they are due**. You are 'solvent' when you can pay your debts and 'insolvent' when you cannot.

For a business organisation – for example a chain of shops, a bank or a football club – the inability to pay debts when they are due means that the business has become **insolvent**. This can result in court action, closure of the business and the loss of jobs. It also means that suppliers who are owed money are likely to lose most or all of what they are owed.

How does all this relate to the efficiency of the accounting and finance function of an organisation such as a business? A business needs to know that it will have enough money in the bank to be able to pay its debts. This means that the accounting and finance function will have to provide accurate and complete information to management about:

- how much money it has **at present**
- how much money it will have coming in and going out **in the future**

Specifically it will need to know accurate details of:

money in:

- the balance of money in the bank account
- amounts coming in from customers and when they are due

money out:

- amounts due to suppliers and for other expenses and when they are due

It is important that the information provided by the various sections of the accounting and finance function is accurate, complete, and on time.

the need for working capital and being solvent

The surplus of

- money in, money due and money that can be quickly realised . . . over
- money due to be paid out

is known as **working capital**.

As long as 'money in, money due in and money realisable' is greater than 'money to be paid out', working capital is positive and the business **can pay its debts when they are due**, ie it is **solvent**. Careful management of working capital by the accounting and finance function is very important if the business is to remain solvent. There are some basic rules to observe:

- pay money (cash and cheques) into the bank account as soon as possible; do not leave it for a long time in the the office before processing it
- minimise the **cost of finance** by borrowing at the lowest available interest rates and arrangement fees payable, and only for the period required

- negotiate 'long' credit periods with your suppliers - ie pay them as late as you can without breaching any agreements, eg after 60 days
- make sure your credit customers pay up on time and try and keep the payment terms as 'short' as possible, ie 30 days rather than 90 days

So, if you pay in at the bank at least once a week, offer 30 days terms to your customers and pay your suppliers after 60 days you are making efficient use of your resources and should have enough working capital to keep you trading.

But problems can arise when there is less money coming in than going out. A new business can sometimes run into trouble, for example, if does not manage its working capital efficiently, as the following Case Study shows.

Case Study

JIMMY CASH: WORKING CAPITAL AND SOLVENCY

situation

Jimmy Cash has recently started business importing home alarm systems. He has put £25,000 of his savings into the bank and negotiated with four main suppliers who have asked for payment of their invoices within 30 days.

Jimmy has been phoning around to sell his products to shops and mail order firms. He is pleased with the response, although a number of his customers have asked for payment terms of 60 days, saying that 'You will have to give me 60 days if you want the business'.

Sales for the first three months go well and Jimmy has taken on two new employees to deal with the volume of orders received. Things have been so busy in this period that Jimmy has been unable to get to the bank very often to pay in the cheques that have started to arrive. He has also received calls from two of his suppliers chasing payment of their invoices and threatening cutting off supplies if he does not pay up. He is also aware that some of his customers have not settled their first invoices. At the end of the three months he gets a call from the bank asking him to call in to discuss his bank account which is now £5,000 overdrawn,

Jimmy asks for your help and advice.

solution

You tell Jimmy that he is in a dangerous situation because he has not managed his working capital properly and may be insolvent, ie he may not be able to settle his debts (to the bank and his suppliers) from the money coming in from his sales to customers.

You advise Jimmy

- to request the bank to allow him to pay off the overdraft over the next six months
- to chase up any customers who are late paying and to bank their cheques
- to try and negotiate a longer payment period from his suppliers

Jimmy has basically ignored the need for careful cash management, and despite running a successful business, is in immediate danger of becoming insolvent.

ORGANISATIONAL POLICIES AND PROCEDURES

The remainder of this chapter deals with the **policies and procedures** set down by an organisation for dealing with a variety of areas, including the accounting function and also aspects such as health and safety at work and employment issues. These regulations are often set down in a series of manuals which should be updated regularly and readily available for reference by employees. You need to know that some of the principles set out in these manuals will be established in law, but you will not need to know about the laws themselves.

We will first describe the **policies and procedures** which affect the accounting and payroll functions of an organisation.

REGULATIONS FOR ACCOUNTING RECORDS

maintaining accounting records – companies

The law relating to limited companies (Companies Act) requires that companies should keep the following accounting records:

- records of entries made of payments received and made by the company and a description of each entry
- a record of the assets (items owned) and liabilities (items owed)
- records of inventory held

These records include financial documents and books of account such as purchase orders, invoices, credit notes, daybooks, cash book, petty cash book and, importantly, a full set of ledger accounts.

This is a description of a fairly standard system of accounting records. An important objective of any company is that this system should be accurate, complete and up-to-date.

accounting records – other organisations

The principles that apply to the accounting records of companies are also applied to other business organisations.

Accounting records, whether paper-based or on computer, should be:

- complete
- accurate
- up-to-date
- accessible – so that information can be extracted for the owners and managers (a need illustrated in the Case Study on the previous page)

retention of accounting records

Another requirement for the smooth running of an organisation is that its accounting records should be retained in accessible form in case of future queries, or even future legal action against the organisation.

Businesses normally have a retention policy stating that records are kept for six years, plus the current year. The reasons for this are based on law. Tax and company law generally require records to be kept for at least six years.

REGULATIONS FOR PAYROLL RECORDS

maintaining payroll records

Payroll records are very sensitive because they involve the rates of pay of all the employees of an organisation. They have to be maintained:

■ accurately – because they involve personal pay

■ securely – to avoid fraud taking place

■ confidentially – because of their sensitive nature

More often than not payroll records are kept on computer. Organisations should regulate access to this electronic data very strictly, normally through the use of passwords issued only to authorised personnel.

The body that regulates payroll (and also VAT) is the government department HM Revenue & Customs, which is normally abbreviated to 'HMRC'. From time to time HMRC inspectors can visit a business and ask to inspect the payroll records with the intention of detecting any tax frauds or innocent mistakes. It is therefore essential that all payroll records – whether paper-based or computerised – are complete, accurate and up-to-date at all times. These records include:

■ wages sheets and deductions working sheets

■ calculations of wages

■ details of income tax and National Insurance deducted

■ tax forms such as P45s and the annual payroll return made to HMRC

■ details of benefits paid to employees such as fuel allowance and other expenses

These inspections are very rigorous and businesses have to provide full details of all transactions and copies of company credit card statements in the case of expenses. If HMRC detects any fraud or major errors it can demand repayment of lost tax and impose fines. The message to staff working in payroll must therefore be that the payroll records must always be accurate, complete and up-to-date and kept securely and confidentially.

retention of payroll records

HMRC require that payroll records are kept for a period of three years following the tax year to which they relate. In other words, employers must keep the current year's records, plus those for the previous three years. It is quite common, however, for organisations to keep at least six years' worth of payroll records, simply because this procedure then ties in with the 'six years plus current year' ruling for normal accounting records.

REGULATIONS FOR VAT RECORDS

maintaining VAT records

HM Revenue & Customs also regulates the UK indirect tax **Value Added Tax** (VAT) which is charged on sales of goods and services and paid regularly by the organisation to the government.

Avoidance of charging VAT – which of course means that the customer has to pay less – is a very serious offence as it is depriving the government of important income. HMRC regularly sends inspectors to organisations to ensure that their VAT records are in order. If they find that VAT has not been charged or paid over to the government, either through fraud or by mistake, they can demand back payment of the VAT that should have been charged and can issue fines. There are reported cases of businesses that have become insolvent because they have not been able to afford the back payments demanded by HMRC!

It is therefore very important that the accounting records and financial documents which involve VAT are complete and in order. Any calculations using the VAT rate must use the correct percentage for the appropriate date, as the government has a habit of changing the VAT rate from time to time.

The accounting records and financial documents involved include:

- invoices
- credit notes
- receipts
- petty cash vouchers
- sales and purchases day books
- sales returns and purchases returns day books
- the cash book and the petty cash book
- the VAT account in the double-entry bookkeeping system

As noted above, it is critical that these records and documents are accurately completed and checked by the accounting staff as a matter of daily routine.

the VAT Return - dealing with errors

VAT due to the government is calculated by an organisation by completing an online **VAT Return** on the HMRC website.

Overall responsibility for the completion of the online form is normally given to a line manager or accountant, but the figures that are entered on it are likely to be drawn up and entered by accounting staff at assistant level. The accounting information includes totals such as:

- sales made for the period by the organisation
- the VAT charged by the organisation on the sales
- purchases and expenses paid by the organisation for the period
- the VAT paid by the organisation on the purchases and expenses

These totals should be accurate and checked; they may be taken from a computer printout or worked out manually. Inevitably mistakes will occur: a big sales invoice may be missed off, an error may be made in a manual calculation. Fortunately HMRC allow mistakes up to a limit to be adjusted in later VAT Returns. Mistakes on VAT Returns, however cost money in terms of time spent putting them right. Large errors can attract fines and fines are also payable if the VAT Return is completed very late, or not at all.

As with accounting records in general, VAT records should be retained for six years plus the current year.

AUTHORISATION PROCEDURES

reporting lines and authorisation

As mentioned in the last chapter, **reporting lines** are an important element in an accounting system. Each employee is placed within a certain level of authority and will report to a higher level which will be given the responsibility of **authorising** whatever it is that the more junior employee is required to do. Typical transactions and documents which require authorisation include:

- authorisation of purchases (the signing of purchase orders)
- the making of payments (signing cheques, BACS payment orders)
- paying in at the bank (signing the paying in slip)
- petty cash payments (signing the petty cash voucher)
- payroll processing (checking and signing the payment instructions)

If the organisation is a large one the authorisation process may be more complex. For example:

- authorising payments (including the signing of cheques) up to £1,000 may require one signature, whereas payments of £1,000 or more may require two signatures

- authorisation of payroll payments may require a senior manager's signature

- a VAT Return may require a senior manager's or director's authorisation

If, however, it is a small business organisation with only five employees, there will be far fewer regulations of this type. It may be that the 'boss' will authorise everything and will delegate this when he or she goes on holiday.

The important point of all this is that employees should

- know what needs authorising and by whom

- keep to the regulations with no short-cuts being taken

The organisation will then run far more efficiently and smoothly. If there are any problems or errors, the person responsible can be identified and the problem resolved and the errors corrected.

Some sample clauses from a 'Policies and Procedures' document for the accounting and finance function are shown on the next page. Read them through and relate them to what you have already learnt.

OFFICE MANAGEMENT POLICIES AND PROCEDURES

An efficient organisation will have well-established and documented policies and procedures covering a wide range of issues relating to staff behaviour and office organisation. They are documented because they should be set out in in-house manuals which should be read by all staff. These include:

- a **code of conduct**: covering issues such as the use of the internet and emails, mobile phones, drug and alcohol policy,

- **health and safety**: maintaining a safe and hazard-free working environment

- **confidentiality**: ensuring security of customer data

- **'green' policies**: saving the planet through conservation of energy and recycling

We will deal with the first three of these in the next few pages.

'Green' policies are covered in detail in the next chapter, which deals with 'Sustainability' issues.

POLICIES AND PROCEDURES STATEMENT– ACCOUNTING AND FINANCE (extracts)

Books of account and records

Proper accounting records will be kept. The accounts systems is based around computer facilities, using Sage and Excel, but manual/paper records will also be used if appropriate. The following records will be kept:

- Appropriate control accounts (bank control, petty cash control, VAT control, salary control)
- Monthly trial balances
- Petty cash and bank accounts will be reconciled at least monthly
- VAT returns produced on the required quarterly cycle

Ordering supplies and services

Budget holders can place orders for goods or services within their budget areas, subject only to cash-flow restraints. All orders of £1,000 or more must be authorised by the budget holder, except for specific areas of expenditure where written procedures have been agreed. Under £1,000, the budget holder may delegate all ordering as appropriate. Budget holders will discuss with the Financial Controller appropriate parameters, plus maximum allowed deviations before the budget holder or senior manager is brought in, which will be documented.

Payment authorisation and Purchases Ledger

All invoices must be authorised for payment by the budget holder, although the actual checking of details may be delegated. The authorising department is responsible for checking invoices for accuracy in terms of figures and conformity with the order placed, that the services or goods have been received, and following up any problems. Finance must be informed if there are queries delaying authorisation or if payment is to be withheld for any reason.

A Purchases Ledger is operated by Finance. All incoming invoices are to be passed to Finance section as soon as they arrive. Invoices will be recorded in the Purchases Ledger within two days, unless there are coding problems. They are then passed on to budget holders for authorisation. Once authorised as above, suppliers will be paid within the appropriate timescale.

Cheque writing and signing

Signatories will only be drawn from senior staff and directors, and any new signatory must be approved by the directors before the bank is notified. All cheques for £1,000 or over require two signatories. Cheque signatories should check that the expenditure has been authorised by the appropriate person before signing the cheque. Salary payments require the signature of the Accounts Manager or Financial Controller, plus one other. Cheques should be filled in completely (with payee, amount in words and figures, and date) before cheques are signed.

Handling of cash

Petty cash will be topped up on the 'imprest' system, where the amount spent is reimbursed. It is intended for small items, up to £20. Anything over this should be paid by cheque where possible. The imprest has a balance limit of £250. The petty cash balance will be reconciled when re-storing the imprest balance, or monthly if this is more frequent. All cash collected from Finance will be signed for, and receipts will be issued for all cash returned.

a code of conduct

A code of conduct will define acceptable and unacceptable staff behaviour. An efficient office will not tolerate behaviour which will disrupt the normal work flow, as in the following two cases:

No employee is to start work, or return to work while under the influence of alcohol or drugs. A breach of this policy is grounds for disciplinary action, up to and including termination of employment.

Using the organisation's computer resources to seek out, access or send any material of an offensive, obscene or defamatory nature is prohibited and may result in disciplinary action.

Harsh rules, however, do not always increase efficiency. Some employers allow the use of the internet or mobile phones in employees' free time at work and find that this enhances employees' work rate and efficiency.

HEALTH AND SAFETY AT WORK

Responsibility for health and safety in the workplace lies both with the **employee** and the **employer**. You should be aware that there are many different laws governing this area, the most well-known of which is the **Health and Safety at Work Act**. You do not need to know these laws but you should be aware of the principles which they establish. Their aims are:

- to ensure that health and safety measures are introduced and observed both by employers and employees
- to specify the rights and responsibilities of employers and employees
- to enable employees to obtain compensation in the case of injury or ill health caused by conditions in the workplace

We will first describe the employer's responsibilities.

Health and Safety Policy Statement

The law requires that every employer who employs five or more employees must draw up a written **Health and Safety Policy Statement**. This document often takes the form of a loose-leaf manual which can be updated from time to time. The Statement must be shown to every employee. Employers then obtain each employee's signature on a form saying that they have read it.

The document (see illustration below) includes all the details of:

- the names of the people responsible for health and safety
- the need for safety when employees operate machinery or handle unsafe substances (eg bleach!) or lift heavy objects (see picture below)
- the need and procedures for employees to report accidents, serious illnesses or fatalities in the workplace
- the forms needed (including copies) for reporting accidents and hazards

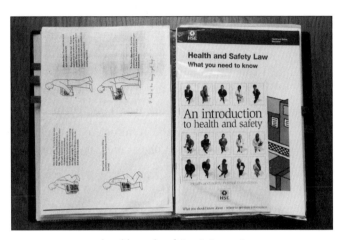

a health and safety statement

the Health and Safety 'poster'

Employers are also required to display a poster produced by the Health and Safety Executive, or provide an approved leaflet which usefully summarise the employer's obligations. An extract from the poster is shown below.

the health and safety poster (extract)

emergency procedures

Employees should be made familiar with the emergency procedures for evacuating the building in the event of fires and bomb threats. They should know how to sound the alarm.

display screens

There are detailed regulations set down for the use by employees of computer workstations and VDU screens. A 'workstation' includes the computer equipment, the furniture it stands on, and the space, light and atmosphere in which an employee works. Regulations include:

- employees must have regular breaks
- employees must be offered eye tests
- equipment and furniture must conform to strict standards of safety and comfort – eg chairs must be designed to provide proper back support

The efficiency of an office will depend to a great degree on the level of comfort offered by the physical environment. A long time without any breaks spent inputting batches of invoices, for example, could cause errors and omissions.

employee responsibilities for health and safety

An efficient workplace also means that employees have to take care over the way they organise not only their personal space, but also the way in which they treat the whole of the office. Any hazards should be dealt with or reported by the employee, depending on what it is. Hazards that can be avoided by employees include:

- electrical problems – trailing leads and cables
- blockages and obstacles to progress – filing drawers left open, waste bins in the way, boxes stacked up in corridors
- fire doors wedged open (ie safety doors that normally swing shut)
- employees taking unnecessary risks – standing on chairs and desks, lifting items that are too heavy or not bending properly when lifting
- using a computer workstation and not taking regular breaks or not using suitable seating

In short, health and safety involves a partnership between employer and employee; each has rights and responsibilities. If both are respected the result will be an efficient working environment.

employee responsibilities for the work area

Employees like to personalise their working environment in order to establish their identity in the workplace and to create a sense of security. Examples of this include photographs, plants and small posters saying things like 'you don't have to be mad to work here, but it helps.'

The organisation may not have formal written guidelines which will regulate the extent to which an employee can put up posters, postcards and other items, but management will monitor the workplace to prevent any excesses of bad taste!

Some modern offices operate 'hot desking' where no employee has a personal desk but has to take whatever space is available at the time. The employee may keep personal files, stationery and other work requirements in a trolley which is wheeled to the appropriate desk.

REGULATIONS FOR CONFIDENTIALITY

Employees always have to take care with confidentiality of information held both in paper records and also on computers (where security is made easier through the use of passwords). For example, payroll information should always be kept strictly confidential and not revealed to other employees.

Also, information about customers and suppliers should never be revealed to outsiders. The only exception to this is in the case of banks who suspect customers of money laundering from drug dealing or funding terrorist activities. Here the law requires that the business **must** reveal information to the police authorities.

As we have already seen, data should be retained **securely** by organisations for six years plus the current year.

the legal position

The **Data Protection Act** is an important and well-known law which protects the confidentiality of information about individuals. It applies to:

- a filing system of records held on **computer** – eg a computer database of customer names, addresses, telephone numbers, sales details
- a **manual** set of accessible records – eg a card index file system of customer details

You do not need to be able to quote the Act, but you should know that it states that personal data must be accurate, kept only as long as necessary and kept securely. It requires that an organisation should not reveal, without permission, personal information about its customers to other customers or any information about its employees.

'GREEN POLICIES' IN THE WORKPLACE

As momentum builds for saving the planet by conserving energy and other resources through recycling, many organisations have drawn up advisory policies and procedures for their employees. These obviously increase the efficiency of an organisation because they save energy costs; they also provide a 'feel good' factor for their employees who are environmentally aware.

important note – confidentiality and 'green' issues

An organisation's policies on confidentiality and 'green' issues are covered in full in the next chapter.

WORKING HOURS

Working Time Regulations

The legislation that governs the maximum number of hours an employee may work is set out in the **Working Time Regulations**.

You do not need to know all the details of this particular law, but it is important to appreciate the way it restricts exploitation of employees by preventing them from working longer than they should.

The point here is that an employee working long hours becomes an inefficient and dissatisfied employee who will detract from the effectiveness of the organisation.

The basic elements of the **Working Time Regulations** are as follows:

- employees do not usually have to work more than 48 hours a week on average
- employees can opt out of this restriction, but only if they want to
- some areas of employment have specific regulations for their own employees, eg the armed forces, emergency services and the police

the Minimum Wage

Legislation also covers the minimum level of wages that employers are allowed to pay their employees. It also covers the minimum level of holiday entitlement. It is important to appreciate that this legislation prevents employers exploiting employees by paying them too little and not giving them enough holiday. This would very likely result in them becoming dissatisfied and ineffective in their work.

■ **Efficiency** in an organisation means achieving the right result with the minimum of wasted time, effort or expense. To achieve this the accounting and finance function must provide information, internally and to other departments. This information should be complete, accurate and on time.

■ **Efficiency** in an organisation is the responsibility of employees and also management.

■ **Solvency** means paying debts when they become due. If there is a shortage of cash there is a risk of insolvency. The accounting and finance function must ensure that management are made fully aware at all times of the cash position of an organisation: cash coming in should meet the requirement for cash going out.

■ Organisations should draw up formal **policies and procedures** which are documents which regulate a wide variety of areas of the business, for example accounting records and accounting procedures, health and safety in the workplace, confidentiality and conduct.

■ The accounting and finance function will be subject to **external regulations**, some of them set down in law, which must be complied with. Failure to do so may result in fines and extra work by accounting and finance staff.

■ Policies and procedures also affect **working practices** in the accounting and finance function. These include internal requirements such as the setting of deadlines, procedures for authorisation of purchases, payments, cheques and details of who can sign different types of authorisation.

■ Policies and procedures also affect the **working area** in the accounting and finance function. This invloves strict regulation of issues such as health and safety, organisation of the workspace and secure storage of documents.

■ **Confidentiality** of information – a concept which is a legal requirement (Data Protection Act) – must be complied with if the organisation is to remain efficient. See also the next chapter.

■ Guidance policies and procedures may also be drawn up by the organisation to ensure that the office becomes '**green**' – in other words environmentally friendly. See also the next chapter.

■ The control of **working hours** (backed up by the Working Time Regulations) is also an important requirement of an efficient workplace. Employees are also protected by the application of the Minimum Wage.

Key Terms		
	efficiency	achieving the right result with the minimum of of wasted time, effort or expense
	solvency	being able to repay your debts when they are due
	working capital	the day-to-day funds that you have available to pay your debts when they are due
	policies and procedures	regulations set down by an organisation for the running of defined areas of activity, eg payroll
	reporting line	the line of communication between different levels and departments within an organisation
	health and safety	the aspects of an organisation which involve both employer and employee having regard for a healthy and safe working environment for all concerned
	confidentiality	the need for all employees not to reveal any information relating to customers and other employees to people who are not authorised to have that information
	data protection	the legal requirement not to reveal without authorisation personal information held on computer or on paper records by an organisation

Activities

2.1 Which one of the following is the most accurate definition of efficiency?
  (a) to complete a job as quickly as possible at all costs
  (b) to complete a job with the minimum of wasted time, effort or expense
  (c) to complete a job exactly as described in the Policies and Procedures
  (d) to complete a job using the cheapest way of doing it
  Which one of these options is correct?

2.2   Which one of the following is the most accurate definition of solvency?

(a)   receiving all your customer payments on the due date

(b)   having a lot of money in the bank

(c)   being able to pay all your debts when they are due

(d)   being able to pay all the wages on the due date

Which one of these options is correct?

2.3   If you want to improve your working capital position you should:

(a)   pay your suppliers earlier

(b)   get your customers to pay you earlier

(c)   pay your wages earlier

(d)   pay in at the bank less frequently

Which one of these options is correct?

2.4   Policies and procedures are

(a)   Company rule books required for the workplace by law

(b)   Rule books for business organisations drawn up by their employees

(c)   HM Revenue & Customs requirements for deducting tax from employees

(d)   Rules and regulations drawn up by organisations to cover different functional areas

Which one of these options is correct?

2.5   The VAT records of a business organisation should be accurate and complete so that

(a)   the business becomes efficient and pays as little VAT as possible

(b)   a complete and accurate VAT return may be made to HM Revenue & Customs

(c)   the annual payroll return can be made to HM Revenue & Customs without any delay

(d)   the credit customers of the business will pay up on time

Which one of these options is correct?

2.6   A Health and Safety Policy Statement is

(a)   issued each year by the Government to help protect employees at work

(b)   drawn up by employees to state their rights to personalise their working area

(c)   a list of the accidents and fatalities at work each year

(d)   drawn up by the employer as a guide to employees of health and safety arrangements

Which one of these options is correct?

2.7   The requirement for confidentiality means that employees of a business organisation

(a)   should only reveal financial information about their own company when authorised to do so

(b)   should only reveal information about their customers when they are off work premises

(c)   should only reveal financial information about their own business six years after the event

(d)   should never reveal to the police if they see that customers are 'laundering' money

Which one of these options is correct?

3 Ethical behaviour and sustainability

this chapter covers...

This chapter covers two areas which affect employees in an organisation:

- **ethics** – the fundamental principles which guide the way people behave
- **sustainability** – the responsibility of an organisation and its employees to 'protect the planet', ie looking after the environment and the people who live in it

Ethics in the workplace (also known as 'professional ethics') are based on a number of fundamental guiding principles for the way employees behave at work:

- integrity
- objectivity
- equality
- professional competence and due care
- confidentiality
- professional behaviour

These principles will be explained fully in the text. Two areas will be given particular emphasis: confidentiality and conflicts of interest (an aspect of objectivity).

Sustainability is a term which is used a great deal nowadays to cover 'green' and socially responsible policies adopted by organisations, for example:

- energy conservation (cycle to work schemes, car sharing)
- recycling of waste and other materials (paper, plastics)
- helping the community (sports sponsorship, charity events)

This chapter will concentrate on the impact these policies have on an organisation, both in relation to public image and also in a financial context.

FUNDAMENTAL PRINCIPLES OF ETHICS IN THE WORKPLACE

a definition

Ethics in the workplace can be defined as:

'the moral principles or standards that govern the conduct of the members of an organisation'.

In other words ethics affect the way in which employees should behave, both in the workplace and when representing their organisation outside the workplace. Ethics in this context are referred to as 'professional ethics'.

As you will see from this, employees do not 'switch off' ethical behaviour when they leave work. Not only do they have to behave in an ethical way in an Accounts Department, they have to have the interests of the organisation in mind when at home talking to the family and when out socially with friends who may happen to have a commercial interest in the organisation, for example as a customer or as a supplier.

the fundamental ethical principles

Most professions – including the accounting profession (and AAT) – have their own written Code of Ethics. These are all based on **fundamental ethical principles**, which are the rules which guide ethical behaviour. You do not have to study these Codes, but you do have to know for your assessment what the following fundamental principles are and how they affect accounting employees. The main fundamental ethical principles you need to memorise are:

1   **Integrity** – which involves honesty, truthfulness and fair dealing

2   **Objectivity** – not being influenced through conflicts of interest

3   **Equality** – treating every person and situation without discriminating in any way, eg in terms of gender, age, race or disability

4   **Professional Competence and Due Care** – developing professional knowledge and skills, and using them to the full

5   **Confidentiality** – when to disclose information held by the organisation and when not to

6   **Professional Behaviour** – to act in a 'professional' way and not bring the profession into disrepute

We will cover these principles in more detail in the first part of this chapter and provide the type of practical examples that might come up in your assessment.

integrity

Employees who act with 'integrity' are:

■ **straightforward** – they obey the rules

■ **honest** – they do not cover up the truth, fiddle the books, or allow anything to pass through the accounting system which they know has not been checked

■ **fair dealing** – they treat everyone on an equal basis, they are not involved in 'shady' deals

■ **truthful** – they do not tell lies, falsify or 'fudge' figures, or mislead customers and suppliers with false information, eg prices, discounts

In short, a person who has integrity has high standards of conduct and expects high standards of colleagues. That person will not allow anything that is incorrect or misleading to pass through the accounting system. The principle of integrity applies equally to major and minor breaches of ethics.

---

examples of breaches of integrity

1 An Accounts Manager takes his wife on a holiday trip to Paris and charges the expenses to his employer.

Verdict: he is not honest

2 An accounts assistant buys herself and some friends some sandwiches and coffee at the local Costa cafe and uses the receipt to reclaim the money from petty cash, stating that it was an expense for 'entertaining customers'.

Verdict: she is not honest or truthful

---

objectivity

A person who is **objective** is a person who sticks to the facts and does not allow his or her decisions or actions to be affected by other people's opinions or influence. Objectivity can be threatened by:

■ a **conflict of interest** – a situation where professional judgement is affected because the employee could benefit personally from a transaction

■ **undue influence** – a situation where someone is putting undue pressure on you to do something that you do not consider professional or ethical

We will explain situations which involve conflicts of interest in further detail on page 38.

examples of breaches of objectivity

1 An Accounts Manager lets a customer pay invoices late because the customer is his next-door neighbour who owes him a favour.

   Verdict: this a case of conflict of interest

2 An Accounts Manager promises to recommend an assistant for promotion if the assistant keeps quiet about the fact that he has found out that the Manager takes his wife to Paris on company expenses.

   Verdict: the Manager is exerting undue influence over the assistant

equality

The ethical principle of 'equality' requires that no employee should show preference for, or discrimate against, anyone in any way for any reason.

Equality applies to situations involving colleagues at work and outsiders such as customers. Discrimination can involve many issues, for example:

■ gender

■ race

■ age

■ disability

In the UK the principle of 'equality' is formalised in the Equality Act 2010. A breach of this principle in the workplace could also be a breach of the law and so employers have to be very wary of discrimination in any form.

examples of breaches of equality

1 An Accounts Manager who is well known for his racist views, has refused promotion to a French accounts assistant on a number of occasions.

   Verdict: the Manager is guilty of racial discrimination

2 An accounts line manager is constantly critical of two male assistants who are nearing retirement and calls them 'dinosaurs'. He is, however, always showing the young female assistants constant attention and gives them more interesting work.

   Verdict: the line manager is guilty of age and gender discrimination

professional competence and due care

Professional Competence means achieving a level of knowledge and skills needed for working at a particular level in the workplace. The more senior the employee, the greater the knowledge and skills that will be needed.

Due Care means that the accounting employee must take the required level of care appropriate to the task that is being done. In other words the accounting employee must provide a competent and 'professional' service.

Professional Competence and Due Care requires that the accounting employee should:

- act **diligently** – this means carrying out a task according to instructions, carefully, thoroughly and on time

- use **sound judgement** in applying professional knowledge

- know when to **refuse to carry out an area of work** (eg payroll processing) if the employee does not have the necessary knowledge or skills

- plan career progression through **CPD** (**Continuing Professional Development**), a programme of qualifications, internal courses and expanding experience

  Note that Chapter 8 has further details of CPD (Continuing Professional Development), a topic that will feature in your assessment.

---

examples of breaches of professional competence and due care

1 An Accounts Manager is preparing some financial figures for a company Board Meeting. He is in a hurry to get off to play golf and fails to check the figures, some of which are for the previous financial year.

Verdict: the Manager is not taking due care in his professional duties.

2 An accounts line manager has been asked to be responsible for the Payroll Section for a few months to cover maternity leave. He has no real experience of this area of the accounting system, but agrees to the request because he is looking for promotion.

Verdict: the line manager is not taking notice of the requirement for professional competence – he will not know what he is doing.

confidentiality

Confidentiality within an Accounting Department is the duty not to disclose information held by the organisation about another person or organisation to anyone else, unless permission has been given.

The type of information that should not be given to outsiders includes personal or business details of:

■ customers and clients

■ suppliers

■ colleagues

■ internal information about the organisation

'Outsiders' who should not be given information include:

■ family members

■ social acquaintances

■ 'cold callers', eg marketing survey companies

Confidentiality is a wide area of study which also includes the Data Protection Act 1998 and a number of situations where information can be given out. These topics are explained in further detail on pages 39 to 40.

examples of breaches of confidentiality

1   A customer telephones and asks a newly appointed accounts assistant what rate of trade discount another customer receives. The accounts assistant tells him that it is 35%.

    Verdict: the accounts assistant has breached confidentiality in giving out details of another customer.

2   A man contacts a business and speaks to an accounts assistant. The man wants the mobile number of a colleague. He says that the matter is urgent and he is a good friend of the colleague. The accounts assistant gives him the number.

    Verdict: the accounts assistant has breached confidentiality in giving out details of a colleague.

3   A sales ledger assistant asks a payroll assistant (a good friend) what the salary of the sales ledger line manager is, as she too wants to become a line manager. The payroll assistant gives her the information.

    Verdict: the payroll assistant has breached confidentiality in giving out internal confidential information.

professional behaviour

Professional Behaviour is an ethical principle which requires people working in accounting to:

■ comply with the laws and regulations that relate to the accounting profession

■ uphold the good reputation of the profession and its members

In short people working in accounting should not 'bend the rules' and bring the profession into disrepute.

---

examples of breaches of professional behaviour

1 An accounts assistant is looking for promotion but cannot find it in his own organisation. He decides to apply for jobs elsewhere but in preparing his CV he states that he has a full AAT qualification. This is not actually the case as he has not yet finished his Level 4 exams.

Verdict: the assistant is making false claims about his level of professional competence and this is not professional behaviour.

2 A partner in a well-known firm of accountants has been reported in the press and on TV as helping a number of celebrities avoid tax by breaching the accounting rules.

Verdict: the partner is guilty of bringing the accounting profession into disrepute as his behaviour is unprofessional.

CONFLICTS OF INTEREST – FURTHER POINTS

problems with objectivity

We saw on page 34 that a person who is **objective** is a person who sticks to the facts and does not allow his or her decisions or actions to be affected by other people's opinions or influence.

One major problem with objectivity is that other people's opinions and influence can often be a major obstacle to ethical behaviour. **Conflicts of interest** can often cloud people's judgement.

The normal procedure and ethical position is that if faced with a conflict of interest, the employee faced with the decision should either:

■ say 'no' to the request when to say 'yes' would not be in the interest of the organisation

■ say 'yes' to the request, if it is reasonable, but **declare the interest to the organisation** when the decision is made (or to be made)

conflicts of interest – examples

Examples of possible sources of opinions and influence include:

■ **family pressure** – eg the request by a family member for an Accounts Manager to employ his nephew, whom he knows is hopeless, an alcoholic and cannot hold down a job

Answer: the manager should refuse as the appointment would not be in the interest of the organisation.

■ **business associate pressure** – eg the request by a customer friend of an accounts line manager to increase the trade discount given to his company.

Answer: the line manager should say to the associate that he would have to refer the matter to a more senior Accounts Manager.

■ **political pressure** – eg the request to an Accounts Manager by a friend to sponsor a left-wing political party charity event; the Manager is a traditional right-wing person and does not like the policies of the left-wing party.

Answer: the Accounts Manager should put aside his political prejudice and submit the request to his employers in the usual way.

CONFIDENTIALITY – FURTHER POINTS

The fundamental ethical principle of **confidentiality** (see page 37) is one of the more important principles for the accounting function of an organisation. The reason for this is that the financial information held by the Accounts Department is of a very sensitive nature. If financial data falls into the wrong hands, the consequences could be very serious:

■ **customers** who are given information about other customers (eg credit limits, credit periods, levels of discount) would object if they found out that other customers get better terms – they would want better terms

■ **suppliers** who are given information about other suppliers may also bargain for better terms

■ **colleagues** may also get angry if their details are released to outsiders, eg personal contact details given on the phone to a stranger who may be a stalker or an estranged partner in the middle of a domestic dispute (these are possibilities in example 2 on page 37)

■ **colleagues** may also get angry if their details are released to other colleagues, eg salary rates, age, home address

- **social situations** are also vulnerable in the event of an accidental release of information, eg careless talk about customers by employees out on a social evening, at the gym or at the golf club
- **family situations** are also off limits – there should be no discussion by an employee of an organisation's finances and commercial contacts with his or her partner or other family members

As you can see, the requirement for confidentiality can become a minefield.

situations where confidentiality can be disclosed

If there were no exceptions to the confidentiality rule, the transfer of information could become a problem, so the person or organisation involved (the subject of the information) can give **consent** for the release of the information:

- an **auditor**, for example, will need access to the financial records of an organisation and so will receive written consent from that organisation; the auditor will then, of course, need to keep those records confidential
- a **tax specialist**, who may need to discuss a client's financial circumstances with HM Revenue & Customs (the tax specialist will need to obtain authorisation from the client before these discussions)

Also note that:

- there is a **legal duty** to disclose information, eg if an employee suspects a client is involved in money laundering
- in some cases the disclosure is in the **public interest**, eg a client who appears to be involved in or funding terrorist activities

confidentiality – the legal position

The **Data Protection Act** is the UK law which protects **personal data** from being released to outsiders and makes it an offence to release this information without permission from the person whose data it is.

The Act covers:

- data about individuals (eg sole traders) but **not** about limited companies
- records held on computer – eg a computer database of names, addresses, telephone numbers, sales details of each customer
- manual records – ie paper documents, eg statements, letters

The Act states (among other things) that the data held must be:

- accurate
- kept securely
- made available on request to the person whose data is held on file (they are likely to have to pay a small fee for this service)

SUSTAINABILITY

what is sustainability?

'**Sustainability**' is a term that describes the need for organisations and individuals to become 'green' and adopt policies which protect the environment, save energy and benefit society as a whole.

The three main objectives of sustainability, the concept of which was established in the 1980s are:

■   economic growth

■   environmental protection

■   social equality

These are sometimes also referred to as 'profit, planet and people' – which is a useful way of remembering the three main objectives.

We are not concerned in this chapter with 'economic growth' or 'profit'. This refers to the need for businesses to make profits to enable the environment to be protected and social inequality (the 'rich and poor' divide) to be eradicated.

This chapter will concentrate on the second and third objectives 'planet and people', ie protecting the environment and benefiting society.

ENVIRONMENTAL PROTECTION AND SUSTAINABILITY

The need to protect the environment and conserve resources – the 'green' factor – is one that is most commonly associated with sustainability. Examples of 'green' policies which can be adopted by organisations include:

■   initiatives in the workplace to reduce the consumption of electricity, eg 'turn off the lights and the computers at night' campaigns

■   energy-saving devices such as LED and low-energy lights

■   the use of recycled materials in the office, eg paper and printer toner cartridges

■   using materials from sustainable resources (eg books, such as this one, printed on paper manufactured from forests which are being replanted rather than being depleted)

■   recycling of waste materials, eg paper, plastic, cardboard

- reducing the 'carbon footprint', eg reducing CO_2 by introducing
  - cycle to work schemes
  - low-emission company cars
  - car sharing schemes
- requiring suppliers to certify their 'green' credentials, eg farmers supplying supermarkets being required to avoid the use of harmful pesticides

the financial implications of sustainability

The financial implications of sustainability can work in opposite ways on an organisation such as a large business:

- a sustainability policy can make the business **save money,** but also
- a sustainability policy can make the business incur **greater costs**

One of the major advantages of cutting down on the use of resources such as energy and paper is that it can **save money**. This means that it can actually pay a business to introduce 'green' policies, for example:

- a business that runs a fleet of fuel-efficient company cars will have lower fuel costs and receive tax benefits for using low emission vehicles
- the policy adopted by some retailers of charging customers for plastic bags – this has the dual effect of providing extra income for the retailer while at the same time cutting the costs of purchasing bags

Both of these measures benefit the environment and cut the running costs of a business.

One of the issues of sustainability is that it sometimes requires businesses **to incur extra costs**, for example:

- ordering packaging made from recycled cardboard and plastics which are more expensive but have been specified by the business to prove its own 'green' credentials
- recycling the packaging used on deliveries from suppliers
- complying with regulations which require modifications to products to ensure that they are environmentally friendly, cars for example

SUSTAINABILITY AND SOCIAL EQUALITY

Another important objective of sustainability is the social well-being of people, not just in one locality, but worldwide. At the time of writing there is a distinct lack of equality and well-being. It is estimated, for example, that 1% of the world's population owns a staggering 40% of the world's wealth.

how can sustainability help?

As far as sustainability is concerned 'society' includes a wide range of people and promoting 'social equality' involves many different ways of helping these people. An accounting department may get involved in all these areas:

- the **worldwide and national communities**
    - sponsoring events (eg sponsored walks and marathons) to raise funds for charitable causes, eg Comic Relief, Cancer Research UK
    - sponsoring sport and the arts

- the **local community**
    - sponsoring local sports events
    - providing work experience to local school students
    - providing prizes for school and college award ceremonies

- the **organisation** which employs accounting staff
    - providing the funds and time off for an employee to take an accounting qualification
    - setting up and funding 'bonding' activities within the department, eg a night out, a white water rafting experience

a high quality product

Another benefit which an organisation can provide for its customers is a high quality of product or service. A product which is environmentally friendly and socially beneficial will help to increase sales and profitability.

CORPORATE SOCIAL RESPONSIBILITY (CSR)

Large organisations such as public limited companies like to promote themselves to their stakeholders as being 'green' and socially responsible. This is known as **corporate social responsibility**. By 'their stakeholders' we mean all the people who have an interest in the company, for example:

- shareholders who have invested in them
- customers who buy from them
- suppliers who supply them
- the local community
- their employees

The way in which companies promote the 'green' and socially responsible image is by general advertising and also by the issue of a **Corporate Social Responsibility (CSR)** document. This sets out many aspects of sustainability.

The Tesco statement of strategy for sustainable development is set out below.

Our seven part strategy sets out clear goals for the business to ensure we deliver long-term sustainable growth. Putting our responsibilities to the communities we serve at the heart of what we do is an essential part of it. By operating responsibly and working with customers, suppliers, expert partners and NGOs our hope is that we can leave the world a better place; a greener, healthier and more prosperous place than when we began.

Examples of Corporate Social Responsibility (CSR) initiatives adopted by companies such as Tesco include:

- sourcing products where possible from renewable resources and where local economies will benefit (eg 'Fair Trade' coffee and bananas)

- ensuring that the supply chain is also actively supporting sustainable development (environmentally and socially) and is treated with respect

- reducing CO_2 emissions from premises and from distribution networks

- staff and customer fundraising

- donation of a percentage of profits to charities and good causes

- providing comprehensive staff training and promotion prospects

- **Ethical behaviour** is based on six fundamental principles:
  - integrity
  - objectivity
  - equality
  - professional competence and due care
  - confidentiality
  - professional behaviour

- The ethical principles should be observed not only in the workplace, but also out of working hours in situations such as social gatherings.

- The ethical principle of objectivity includes knowing how to deal with situations where there are possible conflicts of interest between the employee and the employer.

- The ethical principle of confidentiality is particularly important because a leak of personal information by an employee could be in breach of the Data Protection Act.

- **Sustainabilty** is a concept which drives the policies of most organisations.

- The three main objectives of sustainability are economic growth, environmental protection and social equality. The two that affect the running of organisations the most are environmental protection and social equality.

- Many larger organisations set out their sustainability policies in a published document; these policies often go by the name of 'Corporate Social Responsibility'.

workplace ethics	moral principles or standards that govern the conduct of the members of an organisation
integrity	honesty, truthfulness and fair dealing
objectivity	not being influenced by conflicts of interest
equality	behaving without any form of discrimination (in respect of gender, race, age, disability)
professional competence and due care	using professional knowledge and skills to the best of one's ability
confidentiality	knowing when to disclose information held by the organisation and when not to disclose it
professional behavour	acting in a 'professional' way and not bringing the profession into disrepute

sustainability

policies adopted by people and organisations which are based on the principles of economic growth (profit), environmental protection (planet) and social equality (people)

environmental protection

policies adopted by organisations which protect and conserve natural resources:

– energy saving schemes

– reduction of harmful emissions

– limiting the use of materials

– recycling of materials

– using resources which can be replaced

social equality

policies adopted by organisations which promote the well-being of people both locally and worldwide:

– charitable giving

– sponsorship of fund-raising events

– sponsorship of local arts and sports events

– supporting schools and colleges

– supporting employees

Corporate Social Responsibility

the overall strategy of an organisation promoting all areas of sustainability

Activities

3.1 Indicate which **three** of the following are fundamental ethical principles.

	✔
Professional confidence	
Objectivity	
Equality	
Accuracy	
Customer service	
Professional competence and due care	

3.2 You work in the Accounts Office of a large wholesaler.

Indicate which **one** of the following situations represents a breach of confidentiality.

	✔
You have been asked to send some figures to your company's auditors.	
You email your company's Sales Manager with details of customer credit limits.	
You mention to a member of your family that a shop in the High Street that is one of your customers is having financial problems and is likely to become insolvent.	
One of your customers sends a letter asking you to send sales figures to the bank.	

3.3   The four sentences in the table below represent breaches of fundamental principles of ethics.

You are to write in the right-hand column the appropriate fundamental principle which is breached in each case. Choose from:

integrity   **equality**   **professional behaviour**   **confidentiality**

You mention to your partner that her employer has been refused credit by the company that employs you.	
Your line manager says that he needs another assistant, but the new employee 'must be under 20 as the pay rate will be lower'.	
You 'borrow' £10 from the cash till because you are short of cash for the weekend. You fully intend to put it back on Monday, but you forget as it is such a busy day.	
You hear a colleague at a Friday night pub session in a crowded bar say that his manager is 'useless' and he 'doesn't know how he got his qualifications'.	

3.4   Indicate in the table below which **four** of the following are sustainability policies that a business might adopt.

	✔
A cycle to work scheme.	
A policy of re-using the blank side of A4 white copy paper for printing on.	
Testing the fire extinguishers on a regular basis.	
Put up a notice telling staff to only fill the kettle with the amount of water needed when making coffee or tea.	
Use company cars which have the most powerful engines.	
Suggest a team is set up to do a charity walk in support of Cancer Research UK.	
Make sure that everyone has a regular eye test.	
Recommend that the cheapest packaging material is used to save money.	

3.5   Indicate which **two** of the following statements is true in relation to sustainability.

✔

Sustainability involves keeping sales of products at a stable level.	
Computers should be turned off at the end of each working day.	
Sustainability encourages an employer to pay for an employee to train for an accounting qualification.	
It is best to keep lights on at all times because this will mean that the bulbs will last longer.	

4 Working with numbers

this chapter covers...

This chapter is a practical guide showing you how to carry out the types of basic calculation that you are likely to encounter when working in accounting and finance. The important lesson here is that you should use your common sense as well as your calculator when working out a solution.

These techniques include:

■ *carrying out calculations and using estimation to check what you have done*

■ *converting numbers in words into figures*

■ *using addition, subtraction, multiplication and division*

■ *using fractions to express the part of a whole*

■ *dealing with percentages to calculate a variety of figures, for example:*

   - working out and checking discounts on invoices

   - calculating and checking Value Added Tax on invoices

   - working out the levels of difference between actual and budgeted figures

■ *dealing with averages, for example calculating the average value of inventory held by a business*

■ *using tables to present numbers*

■ *understanding (but not creating) the different types of graphs and charts which can be used in reports to illustrate numbers and trends*

BASIC CALCULATIONS

processing of numerical data

Working in finance and accounting often involves processing large volumes of figures. This may be carried out using electronic aids:

■   a computer accounting program for calculating invoice totals

■   a spreadsheet for processing a budget

■   a calculator – maybe with a tally roll – for adding up long lists of figures, eg the total of customer cheques to be paid into the bank

accurate checking of data – estimation

In all these cases accuracy of **input** of the figures is very important and should be routinely **checked** as part of the office procedures. In the case of the addition of columns of figures, one way of checking accuracy is to carry out the procedure twice, and get somebody else to call out the figures if there is a discrepancy.

Estimation is also very important when you carry out or check a calculation. Does the total seem about right? Common sense is critical. For example, does the admin office really need to order 2,500 pens, or should it be 25?

The situation below is based on a real incident and shows the serious danger of not using common sense or checking figures properly.

> **Online Electronics store apologises for 49p TV error**
>
> Thousands of internet shoppers who bought a TV normally priced at £499 but quoted at an online price of 49p have been told the deal was too good to be true.
>
> The internet store is refusing to honour the website deals and has apologised, saying the mistake in pricing was down to a "genuine internal error".
>
> About 10,000 customers had bought the 32" TV over a Bank Holiday.
>
> But the company has now cancelled all the orders and is giving refunds.
>
> A company spokesperson commented that this problem was down to an unfortunate mistake "while keying in data".

converting words into numbers

Another basic numeracy skill is the ability to convert numbers written in word form into actual numbers, for example:

10.5 million = 10,500,000

This is straightforward, but it is important to appreciate that some of the larger numbers are less well known. One billion, for example is a thousand million. The UK National debt (ie what the UK government has borrowed) at the time of writing was an immense £1,400 billion:

£1,400 billion = £1,400,000,000,000

It is rather unlikely that you will be dealing with figures of this size, but it is a basic numeracy skill to know the meaning of this terminology.

addition

Adding a series of figures is very straightforward in principle, but care needs to be taken:

■ when dealing with figures with a decimal point – sometimes the number of decimal places varies, for example:

45.6 + 67.98 + 95 = 208.58

■ when dealing with figures which vary in size, for example:

23,567 + 74,349,117 + 76 = 74,372,760

As mentioned before, it is good practice to carry out all calculations twice to check for accuracy and then, if possible, get them checked.

subtraction and addition

The process of subtraction is similar to that of addition except that you are deducting figures rather than adding them.

Fortunately the calculator with its '+' and '–' function keys will deal automatically with more complex calculations which involve subtraction, or sometimes a mix of addition and subtraction. For example

■ combining two negative figures, eg

– 2 *minus* – 2 *equals* – 4

■ combining a negative figure and a positive figure, eg

– 20 *plus* + 40 *equals* 20

Again, it is good practice to carry out all calculations twice and get them checked.

using multiplication and division

Multiplication is commonly used when drawing up invoices and credit notes manually, and also when checking them. For example, if you receive an order for 10 red box files which cost £4.00 each, you will produce an invoice which will show: **product quantity x unit price,** ie

10 x £4.00 = £40.00

This will appear as shown in this invoice extract:

product code	description	quantity	price £	unit	total £	discount %	net £
BF-R	Box file (red)	10	4.00	each	40.00		

This is straightforward enough; you just need to make the calculation and check it and apply the estimation test. Does £40 seem a reasonable answer?

The last two columns of the above invoice, which include a percentage discount column, are left blank for now. We will explain how to calculate discounts later in this chapter. The use of percentage calculations in business is very common and is explained in the next section.

Division can be seen as the opposite of multiplication. Division works out how many times one number is contained in another number. For example if a business receives 12 bottles of wine as a present and they have to be shared equally by 6 employees, the answer is that they will receive 2 bottles each. The calculation here is very simple:

12 ÷ 6 = 2 bottles each

Division is commonly used in accounting when working out the cost of a product: the cost is divided by the number of units to produce a unit cost. Division also forms the basis of fraction and percentage calculations, as will be explained on the next few pages.

fractions

A fraction is used to express a part of a whole (unit).

- an example of a fraction is $^3/_4$

- the number above the line (the numerator) is the number of parts involved – here it is 3 parts

- the number below the line (the denominator) is the number of equal parts into which the unit is divided – here it is 4 parts

calculations using fractions

If you need to work out a 'part of a whole' using a fraction you:

■ multiply the whole amount by the number on the top of the fraction

■ divide the result of this by the number on the bottom of the fraction

For example, if you need to work out $^3/_4$ of £12.00 the calculation is:

■ 3 (ie the number on the top of the fraction) x £12.00 = £36.00

■ £36.00 ÷ 4 (ie the number on the bottom of the fraction) = £9.00

So $^3/_4$ of £12.00 is £9.00.

As a fraction is a 'part of a whole' it can be used to calculate a sum of money which is included in a total amount. For example, you may want to know how much VAT charged at 20% is included in a £24 purchase so that you can enter the VAT in the accounts. The fraction used here is $^1/_6$. This is known as the 'VAT fraction'. The calculation is:

$$\frac{1}{6} \quad x \ £24 = \frac{£24}{6} = £4 \ VAT$$

This means that the purchase price before VAT was £20 and the VAT was £4.

ratios and fractions

A ratio shows the comparative number of different items in a group.

For example, if you have a class of 22 students which has 9 males and 13 females, the ratio of male to female is 9 to 13; this is written as:

9 : 13

If one of the females dropped out of the class the ratio would become:

9 : 12

Note that you could divide these numbers by the same number, ie 3, to produce the ratio:

3 : 4

It is normal practice to reduce a ratio to the lowest possible whole numbers, by dividing both numbers by the same whole number.

Note also that you can convert a ratio into a fraction. Taking the example of the class where the ratio of males to females is 9 : 13, you can state that:

■ there are 9 males in a group of 22, so the fraction of males in the group is $^9/_{22}$

■ there are 13 females in a group of 22, so the fraction of females in the group is $^{13}/_{22}$

DEALING WITH PERCENTAGES

definition – a percentage is a part of a whole

The phrase 'per cent' means 'out of every hundred'.

So 50% means '50 out of every hundred.' A percentage tells you what proportion one number is in relation to another. In other words, a percentage is a part of a whole, where the whole is 100. It is the top number of a fraction when the bottom number is 100:

$$50\% \quad = \quad \text{the fraction} \quad \frac{50}{100} \quad = \quad \frac{1}{2} \quad \text{ie, a half}$$

If you go to a party where there are twenty people, your partner might use a fraction and say *'I don't know half the people here'*. The way to work out the percentage of people your partner knows is to divide the number known (the 'part') by the total (the 'whole') and then multiply the result of this by 100. The formula is therefore:

$$\frac{\textbf{the part x 100}}{\textbf{the whole}} \quad = \quad \textbf{percentage of the part}$$

Suppose your partner knew 12 of the 20 people at the party. The percentage of people known would be:

$$\frac{12 \text{ people x 100}}{20 \text{ people}} \quad = \quad 60\% \text{ are known}$$

working out a percentage of a given number

This is a very common use of percentages in organisations. Here you **start** with the percentage rate and use it as a number of 'hundreths' to work out the figure you need as a fraction of a given amount. Examples include:

■ **discounts** – an amount to subtract from a money amount

■ **tax** – an amount, VAT for example, to add to sales

This is done by using the formula:

$$\frac{\textbf{given percentage x amount}}{\textbf{100}} \quad = \quad \textbf{percentage amount}$$

Suppose you want to calculate 8% of £250. Using the formula, the calculation is:

$$\frac{8 \text{ (percentage) x £250 (amount)}}{100} \quad = \quad £20$$

An easy way of doing this is to shift the decimal place of the percentage figure two places to the left and then put this figure in a calculator and multiply it by the money amount. So in this case 8% becomes 0.08 and the calculation is simply:

0.08 x £250 = £20

calculating discount amounts

We will now use the formula explained on the previous page to calculate a discount amount. The invoice extract shown below shows the discount percentage given on the sales transaction. This is most likely to be **trade discount** – ie the discount given to customers who expect a discount as part of the trading relationship.

Calculating discounts involves working out a percentage of the total of the products sold and then **deducting** this from the total. The formula needed to calculate the percentage discount which will be deducted is therefore:

$$\frac{\textbf{sales total (£) x discount percentage}}{\textbf{100}} = \textbf{discount (£)}$$

Continuing the example on page 55 the sales total is £40 and the trade discount is 20%. Applying the formula, the calculation is:

$$\frac{\text{sales total (£40) x discount percentage (20)}}{100} = \text{discount of £8}$$

Note that the discount amount of £8 is not actually shown on the invoice; all you see is the amount before the discount is deducted (£40) and the net amount after the discount is deducted (£32). This may seem confusing, but it is common practice.

product code	description	quantity	price £	unit	total £	discount %	net £
BF-R	Box file (red)	10	4.00	each	40.00	20	32.00

rounding of numbers to decimal places

Sometimes the discount amount will not come out as a precise '£ and pence' figure, ie to two decimal places.

The number of **decimal places** means the quantity of numbers to the right of the decimal point. In money amounts this will obviously always be 2. The calculation may produce something awkward like £91.9324 or £45.5786. In this case the four figures to the right of the decimal point will have to be **rounded up or down** to produce the correct number of decimal places to correspond with the two digits showing pence - ie 2 decimal places. In this case:

£91.93<u>24</u> becomes £91.93 (rounded **down** to the nearest penny)

£45.57<u>86</u> becomes £45.58 (rounded **up** to the nearest penny)

The '**rounding**' rule is therefore:

- start with the right-hand digit of the number
- if it is 5 or higher delete it and add 1 to the digit on its left
- if it is less than 5 delete it and leave the digit on the left as it is
- carry on until you have the right number of decimal places (this is normally 2 decimal places in the case of money amounts in accounting)

rounding to the nearest whole number

When you are told to round a number **to the nearest whole number** look at the number to the right of the decimal point, if it is 5 or greater than 5 the number to the left of the decimal point increases by one, if it is less than five it stays the same.

27.938 rounds to 28 because the 9 tells you to go up

28.345 rounds to 28 because the 3 tells you to stay the same

adding VAT (sales tax) to an invoice

The invoice used in the example on the last few pages is also likely to include Value Added Tax (VAT), which is a sales tax. This is worked out as percentage of the net total after any trade discount has been calculated. Like most taxes, VAT is quoted as a percentage rate, and like most taxes VAT varies from time to time. In this book VAT is quoted at a rate of 20%.

The invoice with the VAT calculation will appear as follows:

product code	description	quantity	price £	unit	total £	discount %	net £
BF-R	Box file (red)	10	4.00	each	40.00	20	32.00
						Total	32.00
						VAT @ 20%	6.40
						TOTAL	38.40

VAT is calculated as a percentage of the cost of the goods. If invoiced goods, as here, cost £32, the VAT (at the standard rate of 20%) is calculated as:

$$\frac{£32 \times 20}{100} \quad = \quad £6.40$$

Important note: if the amount of VAT calculated comes out at more than 2 decimal places, you normally **delete all digits** to the right of the 2 decimal places. This is different from the rounding rule set out at the top of the page.

calculating VAT when it is included in the total

Sometimes you may have to deal with a low value invoice or receipt which quotes a figure which includes VAT at a certain rate, but does not actually tell you what the VAT amount or the cost price is. You may have to calculate this VAT amount and the cost before VAT to enter in the books; for example in the petty cash book.

Let us take an example of a receipt or invoice for £24.00 for some stationery. This includes the cost of the stationery (100%) and also the VAT (20%) added to this cost. The total amount therefore equates to 120% of the cost.

The formula to use in this case is:

$$\frac{\textbf{VAT percentage}}{\textbf{100\% + VAT percentage}} \quad \textbf{x} \quad \textbf{total amount(£)} \quad \textbf{=} \quad \textbf{VAT content(£)}$$

Applying this formula to the total figure of £24.00, the calculation is:

$$\frac{20\%}{120\%} \quad x \quad £24.00 \quad = \quad \text{a VAT content of } £4.00$$

Therefore the £24.00 total amount is made up of a cost price of £20.00 and VAT of £4.00 (£20.00 is £24.00 minus £4.00).

If the VAT rate is 20%, another way of working out the VAT included in a total amount is to multiply the whole amount by the **VAT fraction** of $^1/6$, or more simply, divide the whole amount by 6 (see also page 54).

The calculation is therefore £24.00 ÷ 6 = £4.00.

Note that if the VAT rate changes, so will the VAT fraction.

PERCENTAGES FOR MANAGEMENT ACCOUNTING

The application of percentages to your studies so far has concentrated on basic accounting and bookkeeping, using an invoice as an example. Percentages are also very useful for reporting data, comparing the sales and profit results for different periods, for example, or commenting on the extent to which actual sales or profit results compare with the forecast made in a budget. These relate to management accounting (accounting information for decision making by managers).

percentages for comparison

There are many applications of percentages in management accounting. For example a shop owner might say that:

'60% of our total sales for the year were made in the two months before Christmas.'

This is much clearer than saying:

'£240,000 of our annual sales of £400,000 were made in the two months before Christmas.'

To work out this percentage you need to use the formula:

$$\frac{\text{the part of the whole}}{\text{the whole}} \times 100 = \text{the percentage}$$

In the example above, the calculation is

$$\frac{£240,000}{£400,000} \times 100 = 60\%$$

This is useful, for example, when the business wants to compare pre-Christmas sales with other years:

'60% of our sales this year were made in the two months before Christmas; this compares with a figure of 55% for last year.'

This gives you a much clearer picture than if you said:

'£240,000 of our annual sales of £400,000 were made in the two months before Christmas; this compares with £192,500 out of a total of £350,000 made last year.'

This will only give you a headache.

percentages and benchmarks

If you are studying basic costing you will know that a **benchmark** is a forecast figure which is set as a **target** by an organisation for sales or costs for a future period, for example the next year. When the end of that period is reached the organisation will compare

■   the actual results, and

■   the benchmark forecast

The difference between the two figures will then be calculated. This difference can be stated by means of an amount or a percentage of the benchmark (forecast) figure. If the amount or percentage is greater than what would be expected, it will need to be reported to management so that action can be taken if necessary.

The example shown below shows a comparison of two years' sales figures for a business which sells modern art pictures. Study the table and read the notes and conclusion that follow.

ART WORLD LIMITED – Annual Sales				
	Forecast (benchmark) £	**Actual £**	**Difference £**	**Percentage difference**
Year 1	400,000	420,000	+ 20,000	5%
Year 2	420,000	407,400	– 12,600	3%

Workings:

- the first column of figures shows the forecast target sales figures
- the second column of figures shows the actual results for the year
- the third column shows the difference between the forecast and actual figures (a '+' means more than forecast, a '–' means less than forecast)
- the last column shows the difference shown as a **percentage of the forecast figure** (not the actual figure); the workings are as follows:

Year 1

$$\frac{\text{Difference (£20,000)}}{\text{Forecast/benchmark (£400,000)}} \quad \text{x} \ 100 \ = \ 5\%$$

Year 2

$$\frac{\text{Difference (£12,600)}}{\text{Forecast/benchmark (£420,000)}} \quad \text{x} \ 100 \ = \ 3\%$$

Conclusion

1 **Sales for Year 1** are higher than the benchmark by £20,000.

   The percentage difference for Year 1 is 5%, which means that sales are 5% higher than forecast.

2 **Sales for Year 2** are lower than the benchmark by £12,600.

   The percentage difference for Year 2 is 3%, which means that sales are 3% lower than forecast.

3 Management will take action if they think it is necessary.

USING AVERAGES

A technique which is useful when reporting on a series of performance figures, such as sales figures, is the use of **averages**. There are three commonly-used types of average: the mean, the median and the mode.

which average?

Suppose the finance manager of a kitchen installation business wanted to know for budgeting purposes the average job completion time in days, from initial enquiry through to final installation. He has just received the figures for the jobs completed last month. The figures are (in days):

20, 25, 35, 35, 35, 36, 37, 55, 60, 65, 65

What is the average job completion time? We will look in turn at the **mean**, **median** and **mode** averages.

the mean

The arithmetic mean is probably the most commonly-used and statistically-reliable form of average. It is also known as a '**weighted average.**'

The arithmetic mean is the sum of all the figures divided by the number of figures.

The sum of 20, 25, 35, 35, 35, 36, 37, 55, 60, 65, 65 = 468

The arithmetic mean $=$ $\dfrac{468}{11}$ $=$ 42.5 days

This tells the manager that, on average, a job takes approximately 43 days to complete. This will help him in the planning and budgeting process. Note:

- the result is not a whole number of days – rounding up to 43 is necessary
- the result takes into account all values – if there had been an exceptional job taking 165 days instead of 65, the result will have been a mean average of $568 \div 11 = 51.6$ days, a possibly distorted result

the median

The median is the value of the middle figure in a series of figures.

Note that if there is no middle figure, as with an even number of values, the median is the arithmetic mean of the two figures nearest to the middle.

Here the median is 20, 25, 35, 35, 35, **36**, 37, 55, 60, 65, 65 = 36 days.

This will not be as helpful to the manager as the mean in this context; it is useful because it is not distorted by extreme values (eg 185 days) – the mean, however, is more reliable because an equal weighting is given to each value.

the mode

The mode is the value that occurs most often in a series.

In this case the most common period is 35 days (3 jobs), followed closely by 65 days (2 jobs). Note that these two time periods are very widely dispersed. This would suggest that this type of average is not as helpful in the planning process. The mode is more useful in areas such as market research in answering questions such as 'How much do people on average spend on a fast food meal?' or 'What is the most commonly-occurring size of T shirt?'

using the mean in inventory valuation

If you are studying costing you will know that it is important for a business organisation to be able to calculate its inventory value, ie the valuation of all the materials and items it holds. One method of inventory valuation is **AVCO** (short for **AV**erage **CO**st). It is very useful for inventory that is added to from time to time and mixed up with existing inventory.

Take, for example, a business importing and selling Chinese tennis rackets. It buys in its tennis rackets every month and stores them in the warehouse. Because the cost price of the rackets varies each month (due to currency fluctuations) and because the rackets are mixed up with rackets already held in inventory it becomes virtually impossible to value the rackets **unless an average cost is taken**, using the mean (weighted average) method.

The formula for this is:

$$\frac{\textbf{total cost of inventory held}}{\textbf{number of inventory items held}} = \textbf{average cost of an item of inventory}$$

If the total cost of the rackets held is £110,000 (different prices paid for consignments on different invoices over six months) and the number of rackets held is 5,500, the **average cost price** can be worked out as follows:

$$\frac{\textbf{£110,000} \text{ (cost of items)}}{\textbf{5,500} \text{ (number of items)}} = \textbf{£20} \text{ (average cost of item of inventory)}$$

In other words at the time that this calculation was made each racket in the warehouse had cost the business, on average, £20.

The business can then use this figure to work out its selling price and make sure that it makes a profit.

USING TABLES

Tables of figures are often used in accounting and finance for setting out data which is useful to management. Sometimes they can be incorporated into a report (see next chapter) to:

■ provide information

■ illustrate a proposal

Figures in a table which covers an extended period of time (eg 'this year' and 'last year') can usefully provide a comparison for sales, costs and profit. The technical term for this type of comparison of numbers over time is **time series analysis**.

Staff working in accounting and finance will need to know how to set out a table so that it is clear and accurate. The most common way of doing this is to use a computer spreadsheet or word processing program. A spreadsheet will also enable graphs and charts to be extracted; these can then be included in a report to illustrate data and trends.

constructing a table

If you are processing a set of figures at work you may have to construct a table; alternatively the table may be in 'pro-forma' form (ready made) or it may be output from a computer information system, be completed as a computer spreadsheet or as a function in Microsoft Word.

The example shown below shows the sales and profit results for a limited company over a period of four years. Study the table and read the notes that follow.

Amico Ltd: Sales and Profit Statement Report				
	Year 1 *£000s*	**Year 2** *£000s*	**Year 3** *£000s*	**Year 4** *£000s*
Sales	500	970	1,430	1,912
Net profit	65	95	132	147

■ the title clearly sets out what the data is

■ each time period is shown in a vertical column

■ each time period is clearly headed up (it could be a year, a month or a week)

- the units for the data are stated below the time period – here £000s are chosen to prevent the table being cluttered up with unnecessary zeros
- the types of data are set out in two rows and labelled in the left-hand column – ie 'Sales' and 'Net Profit' (which means profit after all expenses have been deducted)
- lines are added to clarify the table – it is not necessary in this case to draw a line under each row of data as the columns can easily be read across; if, however, there was a large number of columns, lines would be helpful

presenting and interpreting the data

The figures set out in the table on the previous page can be interpreted just by reading them, but a much better picture can be obtained by presenting the data in the form of a graph or chart which will provide a very visual concept of each trend and help the understanding of the report.

This process is usually carried out by using a computer spreadsheet or charting package. The graphs and charts which follow on the next few pages were produced by a simple spreadsheet program.

LINE GRAPH

The simplest form of visual representation of a time series is the **line graph**.

A line graph, which can be in a straight line or a curve, shows the relationship between two sets of data – 'variables'. One variable will always depend on the other. They are known as:

- the **independent variable** – the measurement that is at a fixed interval
- the **dependent variable** – the figure that will depend on the independent variable

A common independent variable is time, and a common dependent variable is money.

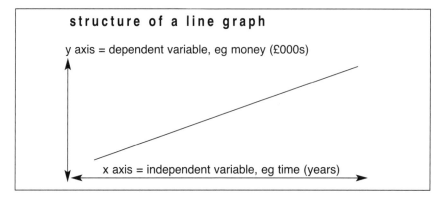

structure of a line graph

y axis = dependent variable, eg money (£000s)

x axis = independent variable, eg time (years)

important note: graphs and charts in your studies
The AAT has stated that students are not required to construct charts or diagrams in assessments. They may however encounter them as additions to reports and other communications. It is important therefore that you know how to 'read' and interpret charts such as line graphs, bar charts and pie charts. The Case Study and text that follows explain how each type of chart can be useful in presenting particular types of accounting information.

Case Study

AMICO LTD: LINE GRAPH FOR SALES FIGURES

situation

You have printed out the sales figures for Amico Limited for the last four years from a spreadsheet and also used the chart function to produce a line graph to show the trend in sales. You then need to explain to a new member of staff what is shown on the line graph.

solution

The line graph is shown below. You have added the boxes and text to set out what you have explained to the new member of staff so that they will be able to 'read' and interpret the graph.

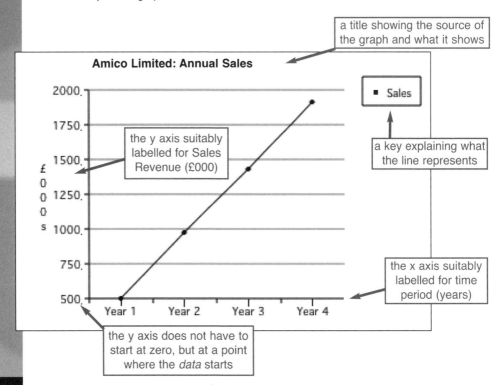

BAR CHARTS

A bar chart is a chart which sets out a series of bars, the height of which indicates the extent of the dependent variable. It is normal to set out a bar chart along the horizontal 'x' axis but the practice can be varied so that they stretch left to right from the 'y' axis.

Bar charts can be simple, compound or component, depending on what data comparisons need to be made.

Most spreadsheet programs will produce various types of bar chart from given data.

simple bar chart

The simple bar chart is the most common type. It works on the same basis as a line graph and illustrates a trend. Set out below is a simple bar chart which uses the sales figures for Amico Limited from the table in the Case Study on the previous page. Compare it with the line graph in the Case Study.

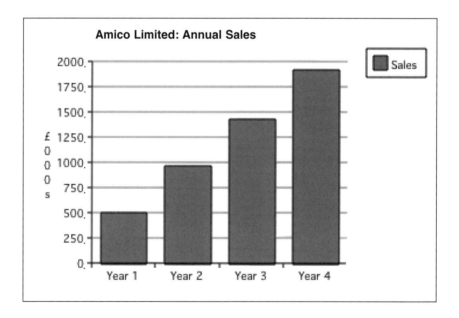

Note that:

■ the labelling conventions are the same as for a line graph – here the bars are shaded in grey

■ the 'y' axis goes down to zero – the whole length of the bar is needed (this is different from the line graph scaling)

compound bar chart

Just as it is possible to have a line graph with more than one line, it is also possible to be given a bar chart with more than one set of data for each dependent variable – eg sales for different types of product. This is known as a **compound bar chart**.

The example below shows the sales figures for product types X, Y and Z for Amico Limited.

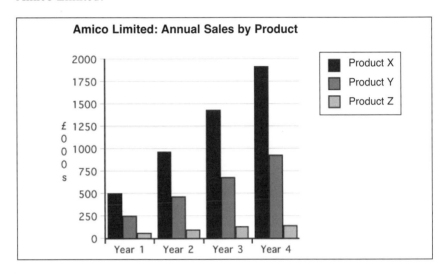

component bar chart

A component bar chart is a bar chart which divides each bar into segments, showing how the total for each bar is made up. For example, if the annual sales totals for Amico Limited were made up of totals for three sales divisions A, B and C, each bar could be shown as having three segments.

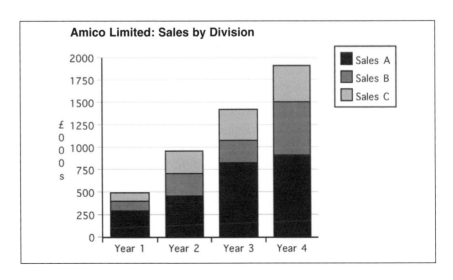

percentage component bar chart

Another way of presenting the sales data is to express the divisional sales figures as **percentages** of the annual sales total in a percentage component bar chart. Each bar is then the same height, ie 100%, and the subdivisions show the trends of divisional sales over the four years.

In the example below you can see that the performance of Division A as a percentage of total sales fluctuates substantially each year, a trend that is not shown on the ordinary component chart (previous page) which indicates a steady increase. This is the type of trend that the management might need to investigate.

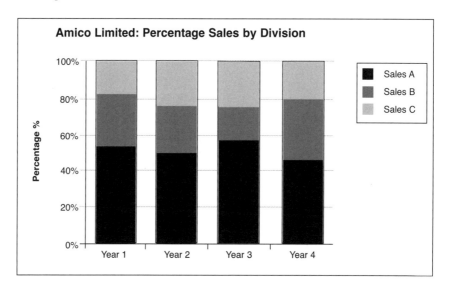

PIE CHARTS

A **pie chart** is a circle divided into sectors to represent the parts of a whole in their correct proportions. It is called a pie chart because, like a meat or fruit pie, it is cut into 'slices'. Most spreadsheet programs will produce pie charts of varying types from given spreadsheet data.

Line graphs and bar charts are suitable for the presentation of **time series** data – data which varies from time period to time period. Pie charts, on the other hand, are useful in showing the breakdown of a whole into its constituent parts **at a particular moment in time**.

If you take Amico Limited's sales figures for Year 1 you will equate the total sales of £500,000 with the whole pie circle. This will be divided into segments, each of which will proportionally represent a divisional sales figure.

The divisional sales figures are as follows:

Division A	£300,000
Division B	£110,000
Division C	£90,000
Total sales	£500,000

The pie chart for Year 1 looks like this:

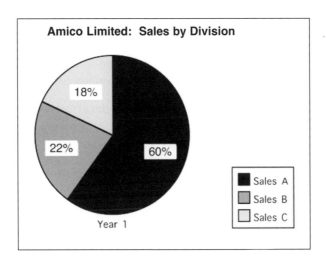

Note that the segments are labelled with the percentage sales. Remember that a percentage is worked out as:

$$\frac{\text{the part} \times 100}{\text{the whole}} = \text{percentage} \dots \text{in this case,} \frac{£300,000 \times 100}{£500,000} = 60\%$$

You may find that you have a report which presents comparative pie charts. For example, the sales figures for two years could be compared as follows:

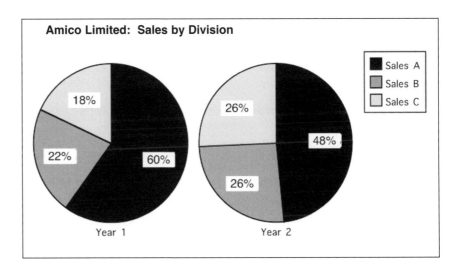

Chapter Summary

- **Calculations** – addition, subtraction, multiplication and division – carried out in the workplace should always be checked for accuracy, firstly by using common sense estimation and then ideally by another employee carrying out the same calculation.

- **Percentages** are based on the concept of fractions and are commonly used in accounting and finance, for example in the calculation of discounts, Value Added Tax, comparison of performance data, and in budgeting for measuring the difference between actual and benchmark (forecast) figures.

- **Averages** are used in accounting and finance, for example in calculating inventory values in the AVCO (average cost) process.

- The **presentation of numerical data** in table format is an important skill for working in accounting and finance. Tables are often incorporated in reports for management, sometimes supported by graphs and charts which illustrate results and trends very effectively.

Key Terms

estimation	using a common sense approach to calculation by seeing if the answer produced seems 'reasonable'
percentage	'per cent' means 'out of every hundred,' so a percentage is the top number of a fraction where the bottom number is 100
discount	a percentage of an amount deducted from that amount
decimal place	the number of digits (numbers) to the right of the decimal point; £ and p are quoted to two decimal places, eg £4.99
rounding	in the case of £ and p, reducing the number of digits to two decimal places by rounding up or down to the nearest p
benchmark	in costing this is a forecast figure for future performance (eg sales) against which the actual figure is then compared
mean average	the sum of a series of figures divided by the number of figures – this is also known as a 'weighted average'
time series	a series of data collected regularly over a period of time, eg annual sales figures
line graph	a visual representation of a time series set out in a line
bar chart	a chart which sets out a series of bars, the height of which indicates the extent of the value that varies
pie chart	a circle divided into sectors to represent in the correct proportion the parts of a whole – like a pie divided into 'slices'

Activities

4.1 You work in the sales invoice section of Wyvern Stationery, a wholesaler. You have a small batch of invoices to process for three different customers. You are required to complete and total the invoice extracts, including trade discount and VAT as required (and rounded down).

(a) 20 box files (black), product code 109BK@ £4.00 each with 30% trade discount

(b) 90 biros (red), product code 235RD @ £5.60 per box of 10, with 20% trade discount

(c) 8 year planners (blue), product code 563BL @ £12.95 each, with 10% trade discount

(a)

product code	description	quantity	price £	unit	total £	discount %	net £
						Total VAT @ 20%	
						TOTAL	

(b)

product code	description	quantity	price £	unit	total £	discount %	net £
						Total VAT @ 20%	
						TOTAL	

(c)

product code	description	quantity	price £	unit	total £	discount %	net £
						Total VAT @ 20%	
						TOTAL	

4.2 You are working out some prices for a customer and note that some discount calculations produce results involving more than 2 decimal places.

You are to use the rounding rules to ensure that all of the following results are reduced to 2 decimal places:

(a) 15% discount on an amount of £45.50

(b) 20% discount on an amount of £44.99

(c) 30% discount on an amount of £21.75

(d) 15% discount on an amount of £390.95

(e) 30% discount on an amount of £964.55

(f) 2.5% discount on an amount of £35.95

4.3 The following amounts include VAT charged at 20%. You are to work out in each case the VAT amount and the amount before VAT was added on.

(a) £49.20

(b) £292.80

(c) £2.28

(d) £436.80

(e) £105.60

4.4 You work for Hypnos Enterprises. You have been asked to complete the following tables showing their annual sales and profit figures for the last two years. You have been asked to calculate and comment on in each case:

(a) the difference between the forecast and actual figures, noting if it is '+' or '−'

(b) the difference as a percentage of the forecast (benchmark) figure

HYPNOS ENTERPRISES – Annual Sales				
	Forecast (benchmark) £	Actual £	Difference £	Percentage difference
Year 1	600,000	642,000		
Year 2	640,000	608,000		

HYPNOS ENTERPRISES – Annual Profits				
	Forecast (benchmark) £	Actual £	Difference £	Percentage difference
Year 1	64,000	67,200		
Year 2	65,000	63,050		

4.5   Shown below are two pie charts based on the sales figures of Newbury Limited for Years 1 and 4.

State why you think these pie charts are not so useful in showing the year-to-year sales trends.

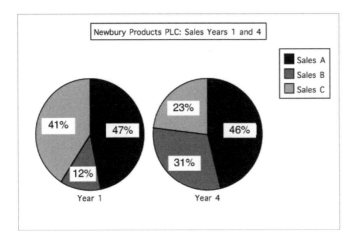

4.6   Calculate the average (mean, median and mode) hourly rate of employees' pay from the following figures:

Andy	£7.50
Bella	£7.75
Carlo	£7.80
Dirk	£7.85
Estelle	£7.90
Freddy	£9.00
Gina	£11.00
Hal	£11.00
Ian	£14.20

Which average figure are you likely to use if you are compiling a report on wage costs, and why?

5 Communication at work

this chapter covers...

This chapter explains the need for people working in accounting and finance to be able to communicate:

- *with colleagues in the workplace*
- *with people outside the workplace – customers and suppliers, for example*

This chapter will explain that

- *effective communication needs to be clear, appropriate to the situation and easily understood*
- *effective communication needs to be accurate and technically correct*
- *when communicating with outsiders, employees should project a professional image of the organisation.*
- *communication may be verbal*
- *communication may be written down by hand or processed on a computer*
- *the language used in business communications is generally more formal than everyday language used with friends and family*

The specific types of communication covered include:

- *emails*
- *memos*
- *notes*
- *faxes*
- *letters*
- *business reports*

THE NEED TO COMMUNICATE

the need for effective communication

We saw in the last chapter that numerical skills are particularly important in the accounting and finance workplace. In this chapter we describe the need for effective communication, a set of skills which are vital not only in the workplace but in all walks of life.

If you are communicating a message to another person or group of people, that message must be **effective** to be successful. It must achieve its aim and be:

■ clear and easily understood – concise and expressed in unambiguous language

■ correct – there is no point in unintentionally misleading people

■ provided at the right time – not too early and not too late

On a personal level, if you are organising a meal out with a group of friends, you will need to email, phone or text instructions giving clear details of the place, date and time and asking for confirmation. You need to provide this information in good time and be available to receive replies. This is a very basic comparison, but the same principles apply to any workplace situation.

forms of communication – the people involved

Communication can be very varied. If you consider a working day and compile a log of all the forms of communication you get involved in you would find that you would be recording:

■ **internal communications** – with colleagues, line managers and anyone else involved in your reporting lines

■ **external communications** – depending on your role in the organisation, this could be with customers, suppliers, the bank, carriers and the local sandwich or pizza delivery company

If you are communicating **within the organisation** you should

■ choose the most appropriate method

■ be polite – even if you do not feel like it at the time

■ act promptly – do not leave things to later, they may never happen

If you are communicating **with outsiders** you should

■ choose the most appropriate method of communication

■ communicate clearly, accurately and promptly

■ present a professional approach

■ comply with 'corporate image' – this may mean using standard letters and forms, or speaking on the telephone using standard 'scripts'

forms of communication – the methods used

There is a wide variety of methods of communication that can be used. There is normally a clear choice for most circumstances, although occasionally it can be effective if a normally accepted method is changed if the circumstances demand it. For example, a telephone call may be more effective than yet another unanswered email in dealing with a potential problem, communication being better than silence.

The choice of communication methods used involve a number of classifications:

- **verbal** or **written** methods of communication
    - telephone calls, voicemail messages, meetings, as opposed to
    - letters, memos, reports, notes
- written communication can be **paper-based** or **electronic**
    - letters, memos, notes, reports, as opposed to
    - emails, faxes, texts

The choice will normally be based on custom, ie 'what is normally done'. The variety of possible methods is shown in the diagram set out below.

In the rest of the chapter we will describe some of the more common communication methods – including emails, letters, memos, notes and business reports.

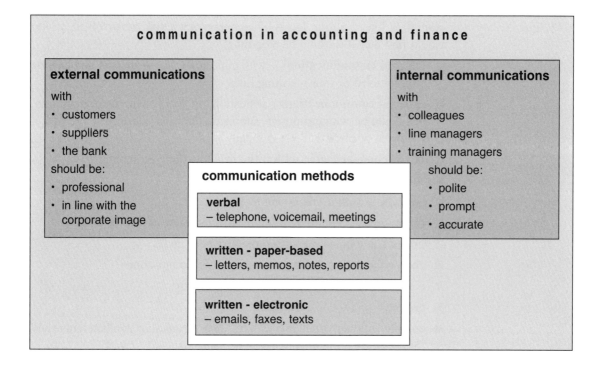

EMAILS

'netiquette' - the art of email writing

Email is a very common form of written communication. There is an accepted set of rules of 'what to do' and 'what not to do' when writing email; this is sometimes referred to as 'netiquette.'If you work for an organisation you must ensure that you are familiar with the ways in which emails are written and dealt with. It is essential that you always project a professional image of your organisation when composing and replying to an email.

Although professional emails are seen as being more informal than letters, there is no excuse for careless mistakes, use of texting language, smileys, LOTS OF CAPITAL LETTERS and exclamation marks!!!!!!!

Study the email shown below and then read the hints that follow.

recipient

It is important to get the email address right.

subject

Keep the subject description short and to the point. Use a capital letter for the start of the first word.

Cc

The 'Cc' (carbon copy) is used to send a message to a group of people, and each person in the group who receives the message will see the addresses of the others in the list. These people should therefore ideally know each other. 'Cc' should only be used if you are happy that they are all aware that the others on the list are receiving the message. If it is used to send a message to a group of strangers you may annoy them and breach privacy regulations.

Bcc

'Bcc' (blind carbon copy) is an option (not shown on the illustration) which can be used to e-mail a group of contacts who do not know each other. 'Bcc' allows the message to go to a group, but the group members do not know that it is a group mailing as they do not see the details of the other recipients.

addressing the recipient

How do you address your new contacts? It all depends on the relationship. If the person is well known to you, the usual 'Hi Ramjit,' 'Hello Laura,' is quite acceptable. The approach is very similar to a telephone call. If you do not know the recipient you should be very formal: 'Dear Mr Lubowski,' 'Dear Ms. Terry,' and so on. You should remain on formal terms until in due course it is clear from the other person that you can say 'Hi Sue,' or whatever is required.

signing off

On the whole you should use the same process as you would if you were writing a business letter. If you start with 'Dear Mr Brown' you should finish with 'Yours sincerely' although there is a tendency now also to use 'kind regards' or 'best wishes' instead.

how formal should the text be?

An email is different from a letter in this respect. The level of formality will depend on the relationship with the recipient. Whatever the level of formality, an email should have correct spelling, grammar and punctuation. Ideally, sentences should be short and separated into distinct paragraphs.

It makes the message clearer if you put a blank line between paragraphs.

If it is an **internal** email, a degree of informality is more normal – eg 'Hi Jon,' 'Regards, Mike' and so on. In practice close colleagues will sometimes abbreviate even further – eg 'John, the Huxborough contract needs signing. Thanks. Geoff.' This type of email is the electronic equivalent of a written note.

For your assessment, you should assume that the email is reasonably formal and follows all the conventions set out on the last two pages.

some email do's and don'ts

Do . . .

- keep the message short and to the point
- when replying, answer the points raised in the incoming message
- reply or confirm receipt of the message on the same day
- read through and edit what you have written before you send it
- make sure the original message 'thread' is included if you are replying

Do not . . .

- use text in CAPITAL LETTERS - THIS IS KNOWN AS 'SHOUTING'
- use too much fancy formatting, eg underlines, different fonts, bright colours – they may be lost when the message is printed out by the recipient
- send large attachments which might clog up the recipient's email system
- say something in an email that you would not say to someone's face

The next form of communication we will describe is the **memorandum**, a paper-based internal document which has nowadays largely been superseded by the internal email.

THE MEMORANDUM ('MEMO')

format

The **memorandum** (normally referred to as a 'memo') is a formal written note used for internal communication within an organisation. It may be word-processed or handwritten, and will often be produced in a number of copies which can be circulated as necessary. A memorandum may be sent by email within an organisation.

A memorandum can be used for situations such as:

- giving instructions
- requesting information
- making suggestions
- recording of opinions
- confirming telephone conversations

A memorandum form is normally pre-printed by the organisation with all the headings in place, and can be half page or full page in size (see next page).

elements of the memorandum

'to' and 'from'   the name and job title of the sender and the recipient are entered in full, and the formal phrases you find on letters, eg 'Dear......' and 'Yours ....' are not necessary

copies to   memoranda are sometimes sent to a number of people; the recipients will be indicated in this section of the document

subject   the subject matter of the memorandum must be stated concisely

text   the message of the memorandum should be clear and concise

signature   a memorandum can be signed, initialled, or even – as is often the case – left blank

enclosures   if material is circulated with the memorandum, the abbreviation 'enc' or 'encl' should be used

---

MEMORANDUM

To   John Stone, Accounts Supervisor

From   Tim Blake, Sales Manager   **Ref** TB/AC/1098

Copies to n/a   **Date** 23 June 20-3

Subject   Bad payers

Please can you let me have an updated list of our customers who exceed their credit period by more than a month and have a history of paying late.

I need to give this list to the sales reps so that they will not be tempted to extend any further credit to these customers.

Thank you.

a completed memorandum relating to customer accounts

THE NOTE

One of the most common forms of communication within an organisation is the **note**. This can be:

- an informal written note, passing on a message or an instruction

- a telephone message (some organisations use preprinted telephone message pads)

The important elements of a written note are:

- the name of the person who is sending the note

- the name of the person who is to receive the note

- the time and date that the note is written

- a clearly stated message

- a clear indication of any action to be taken as a result of the message

Examine the examples set out below and see how they contain all these elements.

To Tim Blackstock,
Order Processing

Please remember to allow PDT Ltd an extra 10% trade discount on invoices this month.

John Tregennick, Sales
03.04.-3   10.30

TELEPHONE MESSAGE

TO   Karin Schmidt, Accounts
FROM   H Khan, Sales
DATE   22 April 20-3
TIME   12.30

Please ring Jim Stoat at RF Electronics – he is complaining that they have not received a credit note for returned damaged inventory (order ref 823423).

Please treat urgently – he is not very happy!

HK

THE FAX

The fax (short for 'facsimile') enables you to transmit electronically an exact copy of the details on a sheet of paper. This can either be done on a computer or on a fax machine. If you use a fax machine you feed the sheet into the machine, dial up the recipient on the inbuilt telephone pad and transmit the document down the line. The machine at the other end will print out an exact copy of the original document.

The fax can be used within an organisation or for external contact with a customer. You normally send a 'fax header' first sheet (see illustration below) and then feed in any further pages/documents as required.

The fax is very useful for sending copies of documents. A frequent excuse given by people who are slow at paying is "I can't pay because I don't seem to have the original invoice". This can be replied to with 'No problem! We can fax you a copy. What is your fax number?' Look at the example below.

Note that the fax is less commonly used nowadays. It is often easier to email the message and attach a scan or pdf of any document (or documents) that the recipient needs.

Winterborn Electronics Limited

Unit 4 Everoak Estate, Bromyard Road
St Johns, Worcester WR2 5HN
tel 01905 748043 fax 01905 748911

facsimile transmission header

To: Jamie Milne, Accounts Office, Zippo Computers

Fax number: 01350 525504

Number of pages including this header: 2   Date: 17 October 20-3

message

Invoice 24375

Further to our recent telephone conversation I am faxing you a copy of invoice 24375 which is now overdue.

I shall be grateful if you will arrange for the £4,678.50 owing to be paid to us by bank transfer within the next seven days.

R Pound

Credit Controller

THE 'HOUSE STYLE' LETTER

When you deal with business letters you will see that the appearance and format of each letter is in a uniform 'house' style, a style which identifies that business, and is common to all letters that it sends. The letter will normally be on standard printed stationery showing the name, address and details of the business, and will be set out with headings, paragraphs, signatures – the 'elements' of the letter – in a uniform way.

There are a number of different ways of setting out the text of a letter. The most common of these – the 'fully blocked' style – is illustrated and explained on the next two pages.

characteristics of a fully blocked letter

- the most commonly used style of letter

- all the lines start at the left margin

- the use of open punctuation, ie there is no punctuation, except in the main body of the letter, which uses normal punctuation

- paragraphs are divided by a space, and are not indented

- a fully blocked letter is easy to key in as all the lines are set uniformly to the left margin

elements of the letter

The explanations which follow refer to the illustration of the letter on page 85.

printed letterhead   The name and address of the business is normally pre-printed, and must be up-to-date.

reference   The reference on the letter illustrated (DH/SB/69) is a standard format

- DH (Derek Hunt), the writer

- SB (Sally Burgess), the secretary

- 69, the number of the file where the correspondence is kept

If you need to quote the reference of a letter to which you are replying, the references will be quoted as follows: Your ref TR/FG/45 Our ref DH/SB/69.

date	The date is entered in date (number), month (word), year (number) order.
recipient	The name and address of the person to whom the letter is sent. This section of the letter may be displayed in the window of a window envelope, so it is essential that it is accurate.
salutation	'Dear Sir. . . Dear Madam' – if you know the person's name and title (ie Mr, Mrs, Miss, Ms) use it, but check that it is correct – a misspelt name or an incorrect title will ruin an otherwise competent letter.
heading	The heading sets out the subject matter of the letter – it will concentrate the reader's mind.
body	The body of the letter is an area where the message of the letter is set out. The text must: – be laid out in short precise paragraphs and short clear sentences – start with a point of reference (eg referring to an invoice) – set out the message in a logical sequence – be written in plain English – but avoid 'slang' expressions and, equally, avoid unusual or old-fashioned words which obscure the meaning – finish with a clear indication of the next step to be taken (eg please telephone, please arrange appointment, please buy our products, please pay our invoice)
complimentary close	The complimentary close (signing off phrase) must be consistent with the salutation: 'Dear Sir/Dear Madam' followed by 'Yours faithfully' 'Dear Mr Sutton/Dear Ms Jones' followed by 'Yours sincerely'.
name and job title	It is essential for the reader to know the name of the person who sent the letter, and that person's job title, because a reply will need to be addressed to a specific person.
enclosures	If there are enclosures with the letter, the abbreviation 'enc' or 'encl' is used at the bottom of the letter.

the 'house style' letter

Wyvern Motor Supplies
107 High Street
Mereford
MR1 9SZ
Tel 01605 675365 Fax 01605 765576

reference ➡ Ref DH/SB/69

date ➡ 15 December 20-3

name and address
of recipient ➡ Purchasing Department
Osborne Car Accessories
17 Pump Street
Mereford MR6 7ER

salutation ➡ Dear Sir

heading ➡ Invoice 8288 £10,589.50

body of
the letter ➡ We note from our records that we have not yet received payment of our invoice 8288 dated 15 September 20-3. Our up-to-date statement of account is enclosed, together with a copy of the invoice.

Our payment terms are strictly 30 days from the date of the invoice. We shall be grateful if you will settle the £10,589.50 without further delay.

We look forward to receiving your payment.

complimentary
close ➡ Yours faithfully

signature ➡ *D M Hunt*

name and job title ➡ Derek Hunt
Accounts Manager

enclosures ➡ enc

TYPES OF REPORT

who needs written reports?

A written report is a way of informing a person or a group of people about a specific subject. A report is a structured way of communicating complex information and can vary in length, complexity and importance. Reports can be:

- short or extended
- formal or informal
- routine or 'one-off'
- internal or external

It all depends on who is going to read it and how important it is. Examples of a less complex **routine report** include:

- a monthly sales report for internal management analysing sales figures by product and region

- a monthly report for management setting out the overtime worked by employees in the various departments of the business

A less formal report may just have a title, date, the name of the person/department that prepared it, the information provided and comments.

Examples of a more complex **'one-off' report** include:

- a **report** to investigate, discuss and decide on specific **policy** issues, for example an assessment of changes to the accounting system, the paying of bonuses, the possibility of exporting products

- a report prepared for a business by outside consultants, eg on health and safety requirements

contents of a report

For your assessment you will need to know that a more complex report will have the following sections (note that they are numbered):

	Title Page
1	Summary (Executive Summary)
2	Introduction
3	Findings
4	Conclusions
5	Recommendations
6	Appendices

REPORT FORMAT

We will describe each of the sections of a report in turn.

Title page

The report will normally be headed up with a single page setting out:

■ details of the person/people it is being sent to (including job title)

■ the person who has prepared the report (including job title)

■ the date

■ the title of the report

For example:

> To: Josh Khan, Accounts Manager
>
> From: A Student, Accounts Assistant, Sales Ledger
>
> Date: 5 February 20-3
>
> REPORT ON IRRECOVERABLE DEBTS

1 Summary

This section is also sometimes known as an **executive summary** because it is written for rapid reading by management (the 'executives'). It may take up less than a page.

The summary will be brief and will set out:

■ the subject matter of the report – in this case irrecoverable bad debts

■ what the report covers – the findings of the investigation into overdue debts

■ conclusion(s) of the report – brief details and assessment of the findings

■ what the report recommends – identification of the debts that should be written off

2 Introduction

This will state:

■ the nature of the task set and the date when it was set

■ the person who set the task

■ the deadline for the task

Continuing the example shown on the previous page, this might read:

---

2   Introduction

2.1   On 30 January a request was made for an investigation into sales ledger accounts that were outstanding for more than six months later than the due date and the provision of a list and details of all overdue amounts. This was so that these accounts could be assessed for possible write-off as irrecoverable debts.

2.2   This report was to be completed by 7 February.

Note that the decimal system of numbering is used. This means that this second section of the report is the Introduction and . . .

- it is given the identifying number '2'

- the sub-sections of the Introduction are referenced with the numbers '2.1' and '2.2'. If there had been a third it would have been '2.3'.

3 Findings (Main Body)

The third section of the report contains the 'Findings'. This is the **main body** of the report and sets out all the information gathered together as a result of the investigation. It lists sources of information and presents the findings in a clear and logical way.

A table could be incorporated to set out the data (see page 63). If a computer spreadsheet program is used, it will give a professional appearance to the report. If the findings include a large amount of data or printouts, they should be included in an Appendix and referred to in the main text.

---

3   Findings

3.1   The information gathered for this report has been taken from:

   - Sales Ledger accounts

   - Aged Trade Receivable Analysis Reports

   It also includes copies of relevant correspondence relating to the overdue accounts.

3.2   A detailed list showing the accounts overdue more than six months is set out below.

---

4 Conclusions

The conclusions should be based entirely on the 'Findings' and should not introduce any other factors or information. This section of the report could begin as follows:

---

4   Conclusions

4.1   The figures and the correspondence in the Findings indicate that it is unlikely that Credit Control will be able to recover the following customer debts:

   . . . (a list of the relevant accounts and amounts would be entered)

---

5 Recommendations

The recommendations are the actions that should be taken as a result of the conclusions reached in the previous section of the report. For example, in the case of the irrecoverable debts:

---

5   Recommendations

5.1   It is recommended that the following accounts should be written off as irrecoverable debts in the accounts.

Sometimes, if the conclusions are brief and straightforward it makes sense to combine the 'Conclusions' and 'Recommendations' sections. But for your assessment, you should assume that they will be separate.

6 Appendices

This final section of a report will include the reference material which is too bulky to include in the main 'Findings' section. In the irrecoverable debt example in this chapter this could include lists of account balances and Aged Trade Receivable Analyses.

---

6   Appendices

6.1   Sales Ledger account balances (as at 31 January 20-3).

---

assessment preparation

You will need to memorise the names of the report sections and the contents of each section. The diagram below should help you.

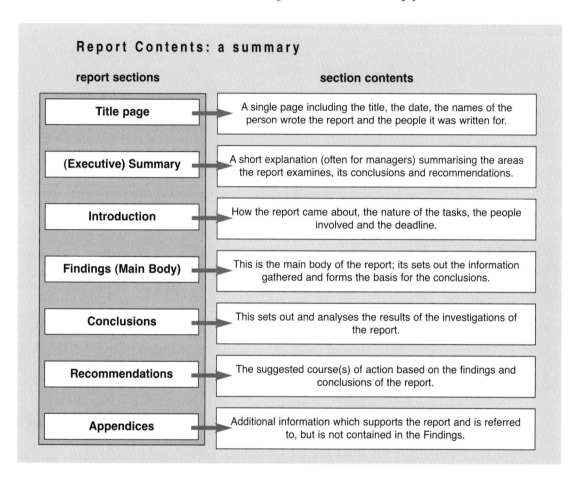

Report Contents: a summary

report sections	section contents
Title page	A single page including the title, the date, the names of the person wrote the report and the people it was written for.
(Executive) Summary	A short explanation (often for managers) summarising the areas the report examines, its conclusions and recommendations.
Introduction	How the report came about, the nature of the tasks, the people involved and the deadline.
Findings (Main Body)	This is the main body of the report; its sets out the information gathered and forms the basis for the conclusions.
Conclusions	This sets out and analyses the results of the investigations of the report.
Recommendations	The suggested course(s) of action based on the findings and conclusions of the report.
Appendices	Additional information which supports the report and is referred to, but is not contained in the Findings.

REPORT LANGUAGE AND STYLE

A report requires straightforward written English. There is nothing particularly difficult about producing written English; the problems lie with the tendency to write as you speak, or as you text, email to friends or post on Facebook. The result is often an abbreviated form of written English which as you will appreci8 does nt work 2 well on the page.

Another problem facing people who are not used to writing formal written English is that they think of it as some sort of overblown 'posh' sounding language which has to be complicated and impressive to make its point. Nothing could be further from the truth. The test of good written English is that it should be plain and simple.

some hints on writing plain English in a report

■ use **simple words** instead of complicated ones

■ use **short sentences** instead of long ones

■ split up the text into manageable **paragraphs**

■ use the **active tense** rather than the passive, eg 'the line manager *carries out* regular checks on the petty cash book' rather than 'regular checks *are carried out* on the petty cash book by the line manager'

■ **avoid slang** eg 'the manager was really *hacked off*'; you should use the word 'annoyed' instead of 'hacked' to avoid the innocent reader assuming that the manager has suffered some terrible injury

■ avoid **abbreviations** such as 'isn't', didn't' and write the phrases in full: 'is not' and 'did not'

Chapter Summary

■ Effective **communication** is essential to the efficient running of an organisation. Any message must be easily understood, correct and communicated on time.

■ Communication in an organisation can be **internal** (with colleagues) and **external** (eg with customers). It is important that all external communications, whatever the format, give a **professional image** of the organisation.

■ There are many different types of communication, all used for very specific purposes, for example:
  – verbal and written communications
  – paper-based and electronic communications

■ The main **verbal communications** are telephone and voicemail messages, and discussions in meetings.

■ The main **written communications** are letters, memos, notes and reports (all paper-based) and emails and faxes (electronic messages).

■ The main sections of a business **report** are:
  – title page
  – summary (also known as an executive summary)
  – introduction
  – findings (main body)
  – conclusions
  – recommendations
  – appendices

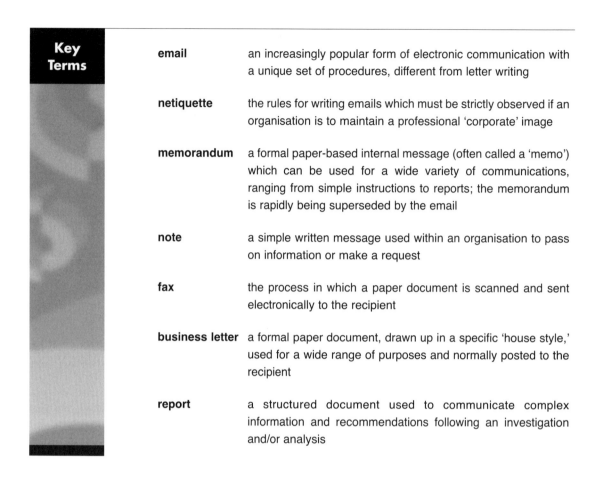

Key Terms		
	email	an increasingly popular form of electronic communication with a unique set of procedures, different from letter writing
	netiquette	the rules for writing emails which must be strictly observed if an organisation is to maintain a professional 'corporate' image
	memorandum	a formal paper-based internal message (often called a 'memo') which can be used for a wide variety of communications, ranging from simple instructions to reports; the memorandum is rapidly being superseded by the email
	note	a simple written message used within an organisation to pass on information or make a request
	fax	the process in which a paper document is scanned and sent electronically to the recipient
	business letter	a formal paper document, drawn up in a specific 'house style,' used for a wide range of purposes and normally posted to the recipient
	report	a structured document used to communicate complex information and recommendations following an investigation and/or analysis

Activities

5.1 Which of the following four options is the most important for creating an effective communication?

(a)   the message must be clear and in writing

(b)   the message must be clear and correct

(c)   the message must be clear and on time

(d)   the message must be clear, correct and on time

5.2   Its or It's? Study the four sentences below and tick the **two** correct options.

	✔
Its rubbish weather today.	
It's rubbish weather today.	
I do not like this film; it's not one of the best Bond films.	
I do not like this film; its not one of the best Bond films.	

5.3   'There', 'their' or 'they're'? Study the three sentences below and if you think any of them is wrong, write the correct word in the right-hand column.

Politicians are corrupt. Their all the same.	
The students forgot there calculators for the assessment.	
They're are sensible students who brought calculators.	

5.4   A senior colleague has been compiling a report for management. He has written each section of the report in a separate Word file and has emailed you seven files which appear to be in the wrong order. The file names are shown below in the boxes on the left. You are to write the file names in the boxes on the right in the correct order, starting with the first file name at the top.

Findings (Main Body)	
(Executive) Summary	
Recommendations	
Conclusions	
Title page	
Appendices	
Introduction	

5.5 You have been passed the following draft letter (to a Miss Coleman) to check. The letter concerns Order No 239847224. It has not yet been signed.

There are five major errors which could include wrong spellings, bad grammar or wrong use of words.

You are to:

(a) Identify the five incorrect words and enter them in the left-hand column of the table below.

(b) Enter your correction of these five words on the appropriate line in the right-hand column of the table below.

Dear Mrs Colman,

<u>Refund for faulty goods (Order Ref 239847244)</u>

We are sorry that you are dissappointed with the goods you ordered from us on 5 September.

They're are two possible solutions to the problem: we can make a refund on your credit card account or issue you with a credit note.

Please let us know which course of action you would like us to take.

Yours sincerely,

---

incorrect word	correction

5.6 Your name is Jamie and you work as an assistant in the Accounts Department of Frankie's Fashionware and have been passed the draft email (shown below) to complete.

The email is a request to Laura Wood (l.wood@frankiesfashionware.co.uk), an assistant in the Sales Department, to provide details of 'St Tropez shades (code 9424)' sold during the month of June. You need the information by 9 July. You are to:

(a) Insert the email address of the recipient in the appropriate box.

(b) Complete the remaining boxes (they are numbered for reference) with the most appropriate words or phrases from the lists shown below (also numbered for reference).

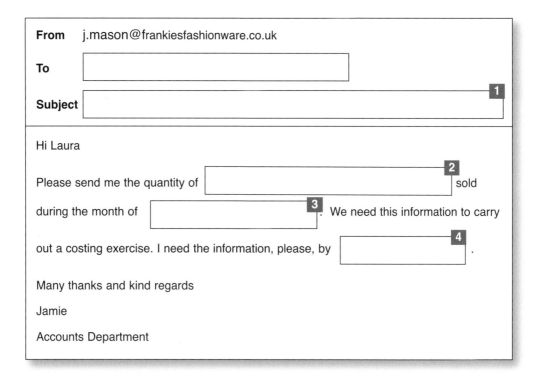

Option Lists
Pick one word or phrase for each numbered box from the following numbered lists:

1 Sales data for June, June data, Tropez data, Shades

2 St Tropez shades (code 9242), St Tropez shades (code 9424), St Tropez shades

3 July, August, June, September

4 9 June, 2 August, 9 July, 9 August

6 Managing your work

this chapter covers...

This chapter explains the need for a person working in an organisation to be able to manage their work in order to help to achieve the objectives of the organisation.

The principles set out here apply not just to the accounting and finance function but to all areas of the organisation.

An employee working as an individual must be able to:

■ *work effectively and efficiently to achieve the objectives set by the organisation*

■ *work in line with the procedures set out by the organisation*

■ *manage the workload by identifying the different types of task involved*

■ *prioritise these tasks and meet deadlines that have been set*

■ *use appropriate planning aids such as diaries, 'to do' lists, electronic planners, action plans and schedules to help with this process*

■ *know what to do if things do not go to plan, priorities change and rescheduling becomes necessary*

■ *communicate with management when things go wrong*

■ *maintain confidentiality at all times*

The next chapter then explains what is required of the individual as a member of a team in the workplace – the need to communicate well and to be able to deal with dissatisfaction with colleagues, management and working conditions.

THE INDIVIDUAL AND THE ORGANISATION

work and family

Employees normally come to work, not just to earn money, but because the workplace, like a family, is a social grouping of people who work and socialise together. By going to work, employees gain a unique sense of identity which the organisation and social grouping provides. The idea of the workplace as an extended 'family' or 'team' was promoted over a hundred years ago in Birmingham, UK, by Cadbury's, the chocolate manufacturer.

Employees in this way learn to treat the workplace as an environment in which they have a sense of responsibility for what they do, for example:

■ the everyday tasks that they have to carry out

■ the idea that they are working together to achieve common objectives set by the organisation

working effectively and efficiently

What exactly do these two terms mean?

'Effective' means getting the result that you want. In football an effective defence prevents the opposing team scoring goals, in the dating game an effective chat-up line will win you the partner you have your eye on. An **effective working environment** will result in the achievement of the objectives of the organisation, for example – a motivated workforce, sales and profit targets achieved or exceeded.

'Efficient' is not the same as 'effective'. It means getting the job done with the minimum waste of effort and resources. This is, of course, an important objective in any organisation. But note that an **efficient working environment** will not always be 'effective'. A line manager, for example, may be ruthlessly efficient in saving time and money, but the workforce may be fed up with her to the extent that levels of performance will fall off. The working environment will become less 'effective'.

The ideal working environment, therefore, is one that **balances effectiveness and efficiency**. The job is done well with the minimum wastage of effort and resources.

employees and objectives

What are the 'objectives' of an organisation referred to at the top of this page? They may well include:

■ customer satisfaction – making the customer the main focus of the organisation

- profitability – which should benefit employees, owners and customers
- being environmentally friendly – reducing wastage of natural resources, eg energy and paper

In order to achieve these objectives, organisations promote:

- customer care schemes
- profit-sharing schemes
- 'green' schemes to cut down on wastage, eg of energy and paper

These objectives can affect the way employees are required to carry out their day-to-day tasks.

The example below shows how a Customer Care scheme in a major financial services company sets very specific targets for the performance of workplace tasks. When an assistant sorts out a customer query, it is not just a case of 'that's another one out of the way' but 'I got a buzz of satisfaction in showing that our organisation cares about its customers.'

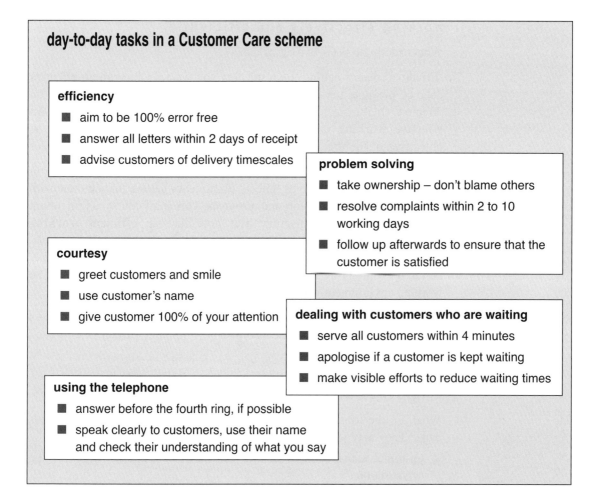

day-to-day tasks in a Customer Care scheme

efficiency
- aim to be 100% error free
- answer all letters within 2 days of receipt
- advise customers of delivery timescales

problem solving
- take ownership – don't blame others
- resolve complaints within 2 to 10 working days
- follow up afterwards to ensure that the customer is satisfied

courtesy
- greet customers and smile
- use customer's name
- give customer 100% of your attention

dealing with customers who are waiting
- serve all customers within 4 minutes
- apologise if a customer is kept waiting
- make visible efforts to reduce waiting times

using the telephone
- answer before the fourth ring, if possible
- speak clearly to customers, use their name and check their understanding of what you say

organisational procedures

The way in which employees tackle tasks is often set down in written sets of **procedures**. Larger organisations are likely to have manuals which give guidance; smaller organisations may have written 'checklists' compiled by experienced staff. Examples of jobs in an accounting context which will have set procedures for the tasks carried out include:

- supermarket cashiers dealing with cash, debit and credit cards
- employees processing payroll
- accounts assistants paying customer invoices

The example shown below is a set of procedures for a shop taking payment by debit and credit card using a 'chip and pin' system.

---

cashier procedures for taking 'chip and pin' payment by debit and credit card

- Insert the card in the card reader, or ask the customer to do so.

- Confirm the amount of the transaction with the customer.

- Ask the customer to insert his/her four digit 'PIN' number.

- Ensure that you are not watching the customer enter the number.

- Ensure that nobody else is watching the customer enter the number.

- If the card is 'locked' at the till, ie the wrong number has been entered three times, the customer should be advised to contact the card company. The customer should be asked to provide an alternative form of payment.

- The terminal will tell you if the PIN transaction is successful or has been declined.

- At the end of the transaction hand the receipt (and the card if you have it) to the customer.

- <u>Alway</u>s ensure the customer has the card in his/her possession when leaving the till.

---

the need to prioritise

So far in this chapter we have seen that an employee normally has sets of instructions and procedures to learn when doing a job. The day-to-day work will involve a wide variety of tasks competing for the employee's time. These may be routine or non-routine, urgent or non-urgent. The employee must develop the skills needed to identify and prioritise the tasks that need to be done. We will now examine the techniques and aids available to the employee to help with this.

WHAT ARE MY TASKS?

keeping to the job description

An employee needs to know:

- what tasks need to be done in the office
- what tasks the employee is able to do in the office

These are not necessarily the same. Employees should be given a **job description** which sets out exactly what the employee is expected to be able to do. It may be that a line manager puts pressure onto an employee to carry out tasks which the employee is not qualified or able to do. The employee may think 'promotion here we come!' but also may get in a mess and make mistakes for which he or she should not really be held responsible.

One golden rule is therefore to look at your job description and know what you have to do and what limits there are to your range of activities.

identifying types of tasks

The next golden rule is to be able to identify exactly what tasks have to be done and to identify what type of tasks they are, because this will affect the order in which you will carry them out.

There are a number of different types of task, for example, in an accounts office . . .

- **routine tasks**

    These are everyday tasks such as reading the post and emails, checking invoices, inputting data, sending standard letters, answering telephone queries, photocopying and filing. They do not hold any great surprises, but their efficient completion is important to the smooth running of the office.

- **non-routine ('ad hoc') tasks**

    'Ad hoc' simply means 'for this situation'. These are the unexpected tasks such as helping with one-off projects, working out of the office on a special assignment, or helping to clear up after the washroom has flooded. These may hold up your normal routine work.

Routine tasks are easy to plan for because they are predictable.

Non-routine tasks cannot be planned for, and they can sometimes cause problems, as we will see later in the chapter. They call for flexibility and logical thinking, skills which can be developed over time.

As you will know some people thrive on routine and do not like it to be upset; others get bored by it and enjoy the challenges of the unexpected.

In addition, tasks may be **urgent** and they may be **important**. These are not always the same thing . . .

■ **urgent tasks**

These are tasks which have to be done by a specific pressing deadline: the manager may need a spreadsheet immediately for a meeting currently taking place; customer statements may have to go out in tonight's post.

■ **important tasks**

These are tasks for which you have been given personal responsibility. They may be part of your normal routine and other people depend on their successful completion, or they may have been delegated to you because your line manager thinks you are capable of completing them.

working out the priorities

Prioritising tasks means deciding the order of the tasks. Which one first? Which one last? Which tasks matter? Which tasks do not matter so much? The two main factors involved in the decision are **urgency** and **importance**.

The guide to the basic order of priority is shown below. You may, of course, think of exceptions to this rule, particularly with items 2 and 3.

an order of priority . . .

1   Tasks that are **urgent and important** – they have got to be done soon and if you do not do them you are going to let a lot of people down – eg producing the spreadsheet for the manager's meeting.

2   Tasks that are **urgent but less important**, eg watering office plants which have dried out – if you fail to water them straightaway the job still needs doing, but the office is not going to grind to a halt if they remain dry.

3   Tasks that are **important but not urgent**, eg producing some sales figures for your line manager for a meeting at the end of the week – the task has to be done, but it could be done tomorrow.

4   Tasks that are **neither important nor urgent**, eg archiving material from some old files. This task is a useful 'filler' when the office becomes less busy; but it would not matter if it were put off for a week or two.

Case Study

FLICK'S DAY – WORKING OUT THE PRIORITIES

Flick works as an accounts assistant at the Liverpool head office of Estro PLC, a company that makes vacuum cleaners. Her main job is to process the incoming sales orders. She is supervised by her line manager Josie Khan.

She is not having a good week and seems stressed by the workload she has been given. It is Thursday 6 February and things are getting no better.

She has written down her tasks on various bits of paper and has stuck post-it notes on the side of her computer screen, marking them 'Remember!' Her colleague, Kirsty, has written notes to her. She also has her daily routine sheet which came with her job description.

These are all shown below.

SALES ORDER PROCESSING: DAILY ROUTINE

1 Collect mail, open, sort and refer where necessary
2 Open email and deal with queries - refer where necessary
3 Check incoming sales orders and debit notes
4 Check sales orders with credit control lists
5 Batch and process sales orders on computer
6 Print sales invoices and credit notes
7 Check printed documents
8 Agree batch total with computer day book summary
9 Pass invoices and credit notes for checking against order documentation
10 File copy invoices, credit notes and order documentation
11 Answer customer queries - refer where necessary

These are the notes received from Kirsty, a colleague:

Flick - Accounts Manager wants January sales figures asap!

Kirsty 6 Feb 9.30

Flick - we are moving the computers at 2.00 Thursday afternoon - can you help? Kirsty

These are the 'Remember!' post-it notes Flick has stuck on the side of her computer screen:

REMEMBER!
Get instant coffee
for staff kitchen.
Ordinary <u>and</u> decaff!
Both jars now empty.

REMEMBER!
4 FEB
Josie wants printouts
of top 10 customer
activity reports by
end of Friday.

REMEMBER!
Old customer sales
files need moving to
separate filing drawer
some time.

How is Flick going to work out her priorities?

solution

Flick takes a short morning break to discuss her various tasks with her line manager, Josie. At Josie's suggestion she thinks about the priorities involved and classifies the tasks according to how urgent they are and how important they are. She starts by prioritising the non-routine/unexpected tasks:

urgent and important tasks

- The Accounts Manager wants the January sales figures straightaway.
- The computers have to be moved at 2.00 pm that day.

urgent and less important tasks

- The staff kitchen needs more coffee.

important and non-urgent tasks

- The top 10 customer activity reports are required for Friday.

less important and non-urgent tasks

- The old customer sales files need moving to a separate filing drawer.

The non-routine tasks are fairly easily prioritised, as seen above, although there was some uncertainty over whether the staff coffee or the customer printouts had greater priority! But Flick's problem was how to combine the non-routine tasks with the big pile of routine paperwork she had to get through that day. Then there was the filing to do and customers on the telephone with 'stupid' queries.

Josie, her line manager, suggests that she should deal with her tasks in the following order:

1   urgent and important tasks – the January sales figures, shifting the computers
2   important routine tasks – these include processing and checking documentation, answering customer queries
3   urgent and less important tasks – it will not take long to get some more coffee
4   important and non-urgent tasks – the printouts for the next day (Friday)
5   less important and non-urgent tasks – filing (daily filing and shifting old files)

Josie also suggests that Flick compiles a prioritised 'To Do' list of all her non-routine tasks. She can then tick off the items as she does them. This will replace all the notes and Post-it stickers she has all over her desk. It can also be updated as she is asked to carry out new non-routine tasks.

FLICK'S 'TO DO' LIST

1 January sales figures for the Accounts Manager.

2 Thursday 2.00 pm move computers.

3 Coffee - get jars of ordinary <u>and</u> decaff at lunch time.

4 Print out top 10 customer activity reports for Josie, Friday.

5 Move old customer sales files to new drawer, as and when.

USING PLANNING AIDS

The Case Study on the last few pages has shown how an employee has become more effective by becoming more organised and prioritising tasks. The Post-it notes are important in the process, but they are only a start. There are a number of planning aids available to help with organisation, time planning and prioritisation in an accounts office. These include:

■ written 'To Do' lists – as seen above

■ diaries

■ calendars and wall planners

■ electronic planners

■ schedules

■ action plans

'To Do' lists

Making lists of things 'to do' is very common both at work and at home, ranging from the type of list shown above to the very basic family shopping list. It is the organised person, however, who writes these lists on an ongoing basis, possibly daily, incorporating actions which have not been ticked off on the previous day in a new list. In other words, tasks that have not been done are carried forward onto a new list. 'To do' lists can be written on paper, or increasingly nowadays, on electronic devices such as mobile phones and tablets.

'To do' lists may be subdivided to show the priorities of the tasks to be done. Look at the example below.

'TO DO' LIST   1 April

urgent stuff

1   Aged debtors schedules for the Accounts Manager for today.

2   Sales summaries for Costings section for today.

3   Get March statements in the post today.

non-urgent

1   Print out activity reports for overseas customers.

2   Set up spreadsheet for regional sales analysis.

3   Look into venues for staff evening out.

---

diaries

The diary organises tasks in terms of time sequence. They are very useful planning aids and ensure – if they are efficiently kept – that tasks and events do not clash. Diaries can be paper-based or electronic. They can be individual diaries or office or 'section' diaries used for a group of employees.

The traditional paper-based diary with a week to view can be used alongside 'To do' lists as an efficient way of time planning and prioritising.The diary shown below is kept by a line manager.

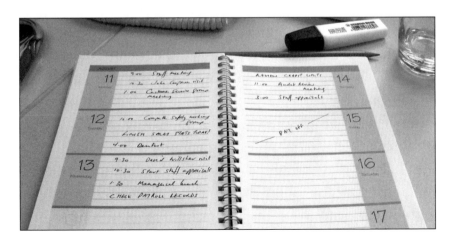

calendars and wall planners

Calendars and wallplanners – often fixed to the wall – are useful visual guides to events and processes taking place in an accounting office, for example:

- ongoing projects, eg installation of a new Sage computer network
- routine activities, eg end-of-month statements, payroll
- staff training, eg work-shadowing and coaching
- and most important of all – holidays

Calendars and wall planners are essentially **team** planning devices.

electronic planning software

The functions of a diary, calendar and prioritisation planner are usefully combined in computer 'planner' software which is available in one form or another on most computers. These provide the functions of:

- a diary
- 'to do' lists
- task prioritisation

The illustration below shows a typical screen from the iCal program available on Apple computers.

planning schedules

Planning schedules are rather more complex planning devices which deal with situations such as projects where:

- some tasks *have to* follow on from each other – to give a simple example, you have to boil the water before making a cup of coffee – these are known as **critical** activities; you cannot achieve what you want without doing them in sequence

- some tasks are **non-critical** – they are important, but the timing is not so crucial – you will have to put coffee in the cup, but you can do it while the kettle is boiling or even the day before if you want!

So whether you are making coffee or planning a new computer system for the accounting department, the principles remain the same. Organisations often use a visual representation of the tasks in the form of horizontal bars set against a time scale to help with the planning. These can be drawn up manually, or on a computer using dedicated software.

action plans

An **action plan** is a plan which will:

- define each activity

- record start and completion dates for individual activities

- state who is responsible for carrying out each activity

- in some cases state the cost of each activity

This form of plan is a form of checklist which can be regularly monitored and amended as required. Plans rarely go according 'to plan'. Computer spreadsheets are often used for setting out action plans because they can be easily amended and printed out in revised form. An extract from an action plan is shown below.

marketing action plan

Product 247G - launch date April

Month	Activity	Person in charge	completed	budget £	actual £
Feb	Book press adverts - trade magazines	RP	6 Feb	5,600	5,750
Feb	Leaflet design	HG	12 Feb	1,200	1,200
Feb	Catalogue design	HG	12 Feb	2,400	2,750
March	Leaflet printing	GF		12,000	
March	Catalogue printing	GF		34,500	
March	Press releases	DD		100	
April	Public launch on 1 April	DD		50,000	

DEALING WITH DEADLINES

what to do when you cannot meet deadlines

Things never go quite according to plan. The unexpected can occur and what seems like a quiet productive day can turn into a stressful time, full of awkward decisions. For an accounts assistant an important aspect of working is therefore **keeping the line manager advised** of what is going on and communicating any problems that arise. The manager will want to be the first to know. If deadlines are not being met, changes will have to be made:

- tasks may change in order of priority
- tasks may have to be delegated
- tasks may have to be delayed

consequences of poor performance at work

Non-completion or a bad standard of work can have serious consequences. If you work as an accounts assistant, or a member of a work 'team' it is important to realise what will happen if:

- work is not completed to the necessary standard
- work is completed late
- work is not completed at all

Not only will the individual feel a failure, but colleagues will be let down and the department will get a bad name. If the public are involved, the reputation of the business will suffer. In these days of online reviews of competitive products and services, a poor review can seriously affect sales.

Here are some examples of how an accounting department could be let down and the reputation of the business affected:

- sales invoices not being checked properly, resulting in customers being overcharged
- statements of account not being sent out which will result in customers not paying their invoices on time and the business becoming short of cash
- careless handling of customer credit card details and the bad publicity which follows if fraudulent transactions result

consequences of good performance at work

If, on the other hand, an employee produces a good standard of work and meets deadlines, this will have a positive effect on colleagues, the team and the whole business. It will also enable the employee to appreciate that his or her contribution to the organisation is valued and important.

The following Case Study describes how an accounts assistant faces a number of problems during a working day. It explains how she deals with the problems by communicating with management and colleagues, prioritising and rescheduling her tasks and making a success of the day.

Case Study

FLICK'S DAY – CHANGING THE PRIORITIES

Flick works as an accounts assistant at the Liverpool head office of Estro PLC, a company that makes vacuum cleaners.

The Case Study which starts on page 102 showed how Flick prioritised her tasks on one working day – Thursday 6 February.

In this Case Study we will see how she copes with unexpected events on that day by changing the priorities of her tasks and asking for help from managerial staff where appropriate.

To recap on what Flick had planned for Thursday:

1   The urgent tasks were to provide the January sales figures for the Accounts Manager and to help with moving the computers in the afternoon.

2   Flick had planned to get some jars of office coffee at lunchtime.

3   There was the normal daily sales order processing work and filing to be done.

4   Flick also had to provide some customer activity printouts for the following day and had been asked to move some filing records.

Flick's problems

Flick was faced with a number of problems as soon as she got to work on the Thursday. These meant that her carefully thought out work plan was in trouble and would have to be revised. The problems were:

1   **09.30**. Her colleague, Kirsty, who helped her with her sales order processing work had to go home sick. She had eaten a dodgy curry the night before and was in no fit state to work. There was a trainee working on the invoicing as well, but Flick doubted if this trainee could cope with the extra work involved.

2   **10.00**. Flick saw from Kirsty's note that she had to give the Accounts Manager the January sales figures 'as soon as possible'. This seemed a bit vague. Did it mean during the morning, or would later in the day be OK?

3   **11.30**. Flick's printer jammed and a long run of invoices was ruined. She could not seem to get it to work again.

4   **12.00**. The Human Resources Manager phoned through to ask if she could 'pop in' to see her at 1.45. Was she free then? Flick knew that she had to move the computers at 2.00.

5   **12.30**. Flick realised that she was going to have to work for most of her lunch break. What about the coffee she was supposed to be getting?

Flick was faced with a number of situations which clearly meant that her work plan was going to be disrupted and would have to be revised. But how was she to do this? She obviously needed to make suggestions to the management about what should be done. Some of the decisions would have to be made by the management.

09.30 Kirsty away off sick

Kirsty's absence would mean that Kirsty's routine processing work would have to be done by someone else – either Flick (who was busy anyway) or the trainee – unless it could be left until the next day. Flick would need to assess how much work there was and then speak to the line manager, Josie. The line manager said to Flick 'Do what you can, concentrating on orders from the important customers. The rest will have to wait. I don't think the trainee can be left on her own yet.' Flick was not too happy about this because she was very busy herself. She would have to put some of her other tasks back in order of priority.

10.00 the figures for the Accounts Manager

Flick realised that this was a priority job. To clarify what 'as soon as possible' really meant, she emailed the Accounts Manager who replied that the figures would be needed by lunchtime that day for a meeting in the afternoon. This job remained top priority.

11.30 printer jam

The printer jam had to be referred to the line manager who called in the maintenance engineer. Flick knew that the invoices would have to be printed that day, so she arranged to print them on another printer through the network. She lost valuable time in sorting out this problem and only got back to work at 11.50, by which time she was getting really stressed.

12.00 Human Resources Manager

Flick realised that the 1.45 appointment with the Human Resources Manager would clash with having to move the computers. The request, however, came from a senior manager and took priority over most other tasks. Flick referred the problem to her line manager who said it would be OK for Flick to go to the appointment. Flick was secretly quite pleased to miss lugging the computers about.

12.30 ooffee?

Flick realised that she would have to work through some of her lunch hour, which meant that she would not be able to get the coffee. She explained this to Jack, another colleague, who agreed to get the coffee for her.

17.00 end of the day review . . .

Flick is in good spirits because she has had a productive afternoon. Her work targets for the day have largely been completed, despite the changes of plan. The sales figures have been given to the Accounts Manager and much of the sales processing work has been completed. Flick has had an interview with the Human Resources Manager and even arranged for the coffee to be bought. How has this all been achieved? Flick has successfully reworked her priorities and made the most of her resources – delegating tasks and consulting higher authorities where appropriate.

COMMUNICATION AND CONFIDENTIALITY

communication

The Case Study on the last two pages has shown how important it is for Flick to **communicate** with her managers and colleagues. The process of prioritisation does not just mean placing tasks in order, getting stressed and pressing on with them as quickly as possible and hoping for the best. An effective employee will, like Flick, negotiate politely and persuasively with colleagues and superiors to achieve the best solution.

This communication of problems and priorities by employees to management is important because management will want to see the work flow proceed smoothly and without any unexpected hitches. In the case of Flick, she communicated effectively with management:

- she emailed the Accounts Manager to check urgency of providing figures
- she reported the jammed printer to her line manager who called in a maintenance engineer
- she asked her line manager if she could see the HR manager rather than help with moving the computers

At the end of the day Flick's targets were achieved – including getting the coffee – through her effective communication skills.

confidentiality

As we have already seen in Chapter 2 (page 27) maintaining **confidentiality** should always be kept in mind when working as an individual in an office: employees always have to take care with confidentiality of information held both in paper records and also on computer. For example:

- payroll information should always be kept strictly confidential and not revealed to other employees
- information about customers and suppliers should never be revealed to outsiders – the only exception to this is in the case of banks if they suspect customers of money laundering from drug dealing or funding terrorist activities; here the law requires that the business *must* reveal information to the police authorities

Also, the **Data Protection Act** protects the confidentiality of information about individuals. It applies to:

- personal data held on computer – eg a computer database of customer names, addresses, telephone numbers, sales details
- accessible paper-based records – eg a card index file system of customer details

Chapter Summary

- An individual working independently should be able to combine efficiency and effectiveness in planning the daily workload.

- Employees working independently should develop the skill of prioritising tasks and be able to plan their activities accordingly.

- A 'rule of thumb' order of priority for tasks is:
  1 urgent and important tasks
  2 urgent and less important tasks
  3 important and not urgent tasks
  4 tasks that are neither urgent nor important

- Employees should be familiar with different types of planning aids and construct their own 'To Do' lists and diaries and be familiar with electronic planning aids. They should be aware of planning aids such as project planning schedules and action plans, but they will not have to draw them up.

- Employees should understand the need to monitor the progress of a work plan over time in order to meet deadlines, and have the flexibility to be able to re-prioritise if unexpected events happen.

- Employees should be able to communicate with management if they need help; they should also be able to delegate tasks if the need arises, maintaining confidentiality where appropriate.

Key Terms

effective getting the result that you want

efficient a task done with the minimum of wastage of effort and resources

non-routine task an unexpected task which is not part of the everyday work of an employee

urgent task a task which has a pressing deadline

important task a task which an employee needs to complete and which significantly affects other employees

'To Do' list a checklist of tasks, made by an individual, which can be ticked off when they are completed

schedule a chart used for planning projects which organises tasks in terms of time and priority

action plan a checklist for a series of activities, listing the main tasks, when they have to be done and by whom

prioritising planning tasks in order of urgency and importance

Activities

6.1 What is the difference between a routine task and a non-routine task? Give examples of both from your own experience of the workplace. (If you have not been at work, ask family and friends.)

6.2 Explain what is meant by the term 'prioritisation of tasks' and state the two main factors that are involved in the decision making process.

6.3 (a) Define the difference between an urgent task and an important task.

(b) Normally an urgent task should be done before an important task. Give an example of a situation where the opposite may be true.

6.4 The eleven tasks below are examples of activities which a payroll assistant may have to carry out in an Accounts Department of a medium-sized company. It is Monday in the last week of the month and the office has just opened. Employees in the organisation are paid monthly, on the last day of the month, which is at the end of this week. The payroll has to be run through the computer on Monday and BACS instructions sent to the bank on Tuesday so that employees can be paid on Friday.

You are to reorganise the list, placing the tasks in order of priority.

- Look at the section diary and compare with your 'To Do' list.

- Send email to Marketing Department asking for monthly overtime figures to be sent through – they should have been received last Friday.

- Check that details of hours worked (including overtime) have been received from all departments.

- Distribute the departmental post.

- Draw up a notice advertising a staff trip out for next month.

- Process the hours of all the employees on the computer. Print out pay details and a payroll summary, including the schedule setting out the amount which will have to be paid to HM Revenue & Customs for income tax and National Insurance Contributions by 19th of the next month.

- Pass the payroll printouts to your line manager for checking, and when approved, print out the payslips for distribution.

- Put a note in the diary for the HM Revenue & Customs payment to be prepared on 5th of next month.

- Print out payroll statistics from the computer for your line manager – they are required for next week.

- Prepare the BACS payroll schedule for the bank to process on Tuesday.

- Pass the BACS payroll schedule to your line manager for checking.

6.5 *Note: this Activity can only be carried out after you have completed Activity 5.5.*

When you have prioritised your tasks in the payroll section, a number of events happen during the day which mean you might not be able to do all the work you had planned.

How would you react to the following situations? In each case explain what you would do and what the implications would be for your work plan for the day.

Remember that you can ask for help from colleagues or refer difficulties to a higher authority.

(a) You get a call from Reception at 9.30, saying that your car in the car park has still got its lights on.

(b) At 10.30 the Human Resources Manager calls to ask if you would like to sit in on a Quality Circle meeting at 14.00 to discuss Customer Service.

(c) You get a call from reception at 11.30 saying that a friend has called and wants to talk on a personal matter.

(d) When you are processing the email from Admin Department giving overtime hours, you notice that two employees are recorded as having worked 50 hours overtime. The normal maximum is 5 hours.

(e) The computer system crashes, just as you are finishing processing the payroll.

6.6 You work in an accounts office and together with a full-time colleague work on the order processing and invoicing. One morning your colleague telephones in to say that because of a major domestic problem she is unable to come in that day. Your line manager has said that she can have the day off. The colleague has a pile of purchase orders on her desk which need checking before processing and invoicing, but the line manager, who is a bit stressed that morning, has not asked you to do anything about your colleague's work.

Select and tick the most appropriate action to be taken.

	✔
Carry on with your own work and hope that your colleague will come in tomorrow and clear up the backlog.	
Process your colleague's work as quickly as possible before doing your own tasks. This may mean missing out some of the routine checks that are normally made.	
Carry on with your own work until you have the opportunity to refer the problem to your line manager when she is free.	
Refer the problem to the Senior Finance Manager and say that your line manager is too stressed to deal with the problem.	

6.7   You will encounter a variety of tasks in an accounts office. They can be classified as follows:

urgent   **non-urgent**   **one-off 'ad hoc'**

Complete the following table with the correct classification of task from the above three terms.

Your line manager asks you for the balances of your top 20 customer accounts. She needs the information for a meeting that morning.	
Your line manager asks you to provide information from the office for the accountants who are coming in next week to audit the accounts. You have never done this before as this is normally a senior colleague's responsibility.	
Your colleague reminds you that it is your turn to get the milk from Tesco Express and remarks that the milk has run out.	

6.8   There are a number of planning aids that can be found in an accounting office:

action plan   **'to do' list**   **diary**   **wall planner**

Complete the following table with the appropriate planning aid for each situation.

An employee's personal record of tasks and events over a long period of time.	
A detailed plan which involves a number of people and interrelated tasks and events for a specific purpose over a period of time.	
An annual guide which can be used to display staff holidays and external training courses.	
An employee's daily personal record of tasks to be done in the short term.	

7 Working as a member of an effective team

this chapter covers...

This chapter explains the need for a person working in an organisation to work as a member of a team and make that team an effective team.

Team members must be able to:

- *identify what they have to do in practical terms to contribute to the work of the team*

- *keep to a plan*

- *keep to deadlines that have been set*

- *appreciate the consequences of not completing tasks that they have been set*

- *appreciate the consequences to the team and the organisation of not completing tasks within the deadlines that have been set*

Team members must also be able to know what to do when there is dissatisfaction within the team. They must be able to:

- *identify situations where dissatisfaction can arise within a team, for example problems with:*
  - *working conditions*
  - *styles and methods of working*
  - *management*
  - *personality clashes*

- *identify situations where team members can resolve a problem themselves or where the problem needs to be referred to a higher authority for sorting out*

TEAMWORK

what is a team?

Working with others implies the need for teamwork. It is easy to start to define a team by giving examples – a football team, a workplace team – and explaining that they work together – sometimes well and sometimes not quite so well.

But what exactly is a team?

A team is a group of people working together to achieve defined objectives in an effective way.

In the workplace a team is usually a department or 'section' working in a specific part of an office – eg a payroll section or a sales ledger section. The objective of this 'team' will be to complete the required work . . .

- to a **high standard**
- within the required **deadlines**
- **efficiently** – not wasting any effort or resources
- **effectively** – achieving the objectives of the tasks that have been set (eg issuing all customer statements by the end of the month)

the characteristics of an effective team

An effective team should ideally have:

- a **team leader** who is experienced, respected and motivational
- a shared **common purpose**
- **motivation**: people get a 'buzz' out of working in a team – it gets people going and brings its rewards when the team is successful
- clearly defined **roles and responsibilities**
- good **channels of communication**
- **shared values** – ie a common motivation to work well and as part of a team
- **pooling of complementary skills and abilities:** some people are better at some tasks and some are better at others, and so a team will take advantage of individual strengths and overcome individual weaknesses
- **creative thinking**: working with other people means that individuals can be stimulated to create and share ideas on a scale that would probably not be possible if they were working on their own
- **help and support**: team members usually support each other when support is needed – this can take the form of advice, moral support and assisting with or taking over tasks which may be causing a problem

problems with teamwork

Dissatisfaction can arise within a team. When this happens, the team members will have to sort out the situation, and if they are unable to do so, the problem will have to be referred to a higher authority. Problems with teamwork are covered later in this chapter (see next page).

working at teamwork

Teamwork requires that team members are dedicated to achieving the team objective. This means that team members should:

- be committed to the work of the team
- understand their role in the team and the tasks they are allotted
- take full responsibility for what they do
- assume joint responsibility for the work of the whole team
- take note of and work to the schedules established by the team

the importance of meeting deadlines

The traditional accounting office is set up in a way that nobody is in isolation: the non-completion of tasks by an employee can have serious consequences for the team and ultimately for the organisation itself.

As we saw in the last chapter it is important for the individual to plan out tasks that have to be done and the time that it will take to complete them. This also has to be done to ensure that the team runs smoothly and the organisation is seen to be efficient by its customers.

The following examples show what could go wrong in an accounting office.

the problems	effect on the team	effect on customers
The Sales Manager has asked for a breakdown of sales figures for a meeting he is having with a customer in the afternoon. You put a note in your in-tray and then forget about it.	The team is made to look inefficient and you are criticised by the team members for letting them down when an angry Sales Manager phones up.	If the Sales Manager has not got the necessary information about the customer he will look unprofessional in the eyes of the customer. This will give the organisation a poor reputation.
An invoice is sent out with an incorrect total because you have forgotten to check it. The customer telephones the line manager to complain.	The line manager is made to look inefficient in his control of procedures and the department will also be made to look inefficient. You are criticised by the team members.	The customer will get a poor impression of your organisation and may consider switching business to another supplier if further mistakes are made.

ideal qualities of a team member

In order to create good working relationships, as a team member you should ideally:

■ be pleasant and polite to other team members

■ be prepared to co-operate, even if you do not agree with everything that is decided

■ respect the opinions of others and be prepared to listen to what others have to say

■ ask others if you need help and be prepared to help others if they need it

■ avoid backbiting and criticising the leader behind his/her back

This is an ideal situation, but more often than not dissatisfaction can arise in working relationships and the workplace generally.

DEALING WITH DISSATISFACTION IN A TEAM

what can go wrong?

Dissatisfaction can cause major problems within a team. These problems can either be resolved within the team, or they may have to be referred to a higher authority. Dissatisfaction can result from a number of factors:

■ **poor working conditions** can affect the performance of an individual to a great extent; these can include:

– poor physical working conditions: a disorganised office, long hours without breaks, uncomfortable chairs, lack of ventilation

– psychological pressures: bullying, cultural differences

■ **poor management,** which can take two forms:

– the ineffective manager who does not exert sufficient control or who cannot communicate effectively

– the dictatorial manager who is a 'control freak' and does not allow team members to manage their own work tasks and work flow

■ **different working styles,** which can become a problem if an employee moves to another job, for example:

– a move from an informal office to an office which operates on a very formal basis, with the line manager at the top and different levels of staff with specific privileges

– a move from an office in which everyone has their own defined working space to a 'hot desking' environment where employees work wherever they can find space on a particular day

■ **personality clashes,** which can occur in all areas of life where people just cannot get on with each other; look at the illustration below which shows what can irritate other people at work and cause problems in working relationships

causes of personality clashes in working relationships

I do not like people who are . . .
- inefficient
- inflexible
- rude
- over-critical
- over-sensitive
- sexist

I do not like people who have . . .
- an inflated opinion of themselves
- personal hygiene problems

sorting out dissatisfaction within a team

It is important for team members to resolve problems caused by dissatisfaction at work as soon as possible to avoid matters getting worse. There are various ways in which to do this, and this will depend on the nature or seriousness of the problem:

1　by themselves, if that is possible – the problem may well lie in their own attitude to colleagues or ability to carry out a task

2　by talking the problem over with a colleague where the colleague may be the cause of the problem, eg using their sugar without asking

3　by referring the matter to a line manager, eg needing training in a certain area, replacing an uncomfortable chair which is causing back strain, reporting theft of money from the petty cash

If the problem is one which relates to a **personality clash between team members** – for example 'she's too slow at her work, and always texting her boyfriend' or 'he's a real pain to work with because he's always making insulting remarks' – the problem needs

■ observing other people dealing with that person – do they have the same problems?

■ talking it over with other members of the team – do they think the same way, or is it just you getting things out of proportion?

■ talking to the person involved – do they actually realise how they affect other people?

If there really is a problem – and it's not just you being negative or over-sensitive – then the matter should be raised with a higher authority.

If the working relationship problem is actually one of harassment – for example bullying or someone making passes at you – the matter should definitely be raised with a higher authority. If it is the line manager who is the cause of the problem, the matter should be referred to a more senior authority.

If the matter is very serious, the **grievance procedure** can be adopted. A **grievance** is a formal complaint against the employer.

We will now look at a Case Study which shows how working relationships are developed within a work team, and the way in which problems relating to dissatisfaction can be resolved.

Case Study

SORTING OUT DISSATISFACTION AT WORK

situation

The accounts staff of Hermes Limited, which sells motor accessories, have been experiencing one or two problems recently which need resolving.

The team from the Accounts Department is headed up by Liz, a line manager. She is helped by two accounts assistants, Luke and Ros.

Liz is a line manager, an organiser, experienced at her work and respected by staff.

She has worked for the company for twenty years.

Luke is a mature accounts assistant, a hard worker, accurate and with an eye for every detail. He is not as fast as some assistants, a quality which can cause problems within the department.

He has worked under Liz for three years, but she has during this time criticised him for being too slow at his work.

Ros is a confident accounts assistant, always ready to give her opinion on how to get things done.

She is sometimes inaccurate because she tends to work too quickly.

She is capable of achieving her targets when given help and encouragement.

She leads an active social life which sometimes interferes with her work.

the problems and some possible solutions

A number of problems have arisen in the Accounts Department involving these three employees. These are set out below, together with some suggested solutions.

It must be noted that there is never a precise solution to every problem, but the situations given here are along the lines of what you might encounter in an assessment. Normally the situation asks you to state to whom each problem should be taken – either the person causing the problem, or to a higher authority, ie management.

1 **problem**

Ros is getting fed up with Luke's slow pace of work, particularly when he is checking supplier invoices. He also makes mistakes in his Sage computer invoicing. As a result Ros sometimes has to do some of his work and gets blamed for some of his errors.

possible solution

Ros should speak to Luke about this problem and explain the effect he is having on her work and her reputation (her appraisal is coming up soon). She could suggest to him that he could ask for some training in his weaker areas. If this has no effect she should speak to her line manager about it at her appraisal.

2 **problem**

Ros spends some of her time during working hours on Facebook and her mobile phone, contrary to company policy which prohibits this. Luke is intensely irritated by this.

possible solution

Luke should speak to Ros about this situation and explain that she is in breach of company regulations. If she takes no notice he should make sure that Liz is aware of the breach of the rules.

3 **problem**

Ros is getting eye strain and headaches when inputting batches of invoices onto the computer.

possible solution

Ros should raise this problem directly with Liz. It is almost certainly a result of sitting in front of the computer for long periods when in fact she needs glasses or contact lenses. Liz should be able to arrange for her to have an eye test and suitable glasses or lenses.

4 **problem**

Ros, who is never slow to say exactly what she feels, is very critical of Luke and is overheard by Liz telling a customer on the telephone to always ask for her when he calls because Luke is 'so slow and has no idea what he is talking about'.

possible solution
This shows a complete lack of respect for colleagues and Liz should take Ros to task for this in private. Not only does it show disrespect for a colleague, it brings the department and organisation into disrepute when Ros speaks as she does publicly.

5 **problem**
Liz is getting more short-tempered at work and very critical of Luke. Recently Liz was standing behind Luke and said in a loud voice so that everyone could hear her: 'Come on Luke, a snail could do those invoices more quickly and more accurately than you. Get a life, will you!' Incidents like this are becoming more and more frequent and Luke is getting more and more upset.

possible solution
This behaviour by Liz has all the characteristics of workplace bullying. Luke should bring the matter to the attention of senior management as it is a very serious offence and completely unprofessional on the part of Liz. It may even require a complaint through the grievance procedure process.

Chapter Summary

■ Effective teamwork is needed if a group of employees is to achieve its objectives.

■ The benefits of teamwork include: the pooling of skills and abilities, the opportunity for creative thinking, motivation within the team, help and support from team members.

■ It is important for members of a team to complete work accurately and on time. Missed deadlines or errors reflect badly on the team member, the department and ultimately the organisation.

■ Dissatisfaction within a team can result from
   – poor working conditions
   – poor management
   – differences in working styles
   – personality clashes

■ It is up to each team member to deal with dissatisfaction in the workplace, whatever the source of that dissatisfaction. This might involve
   – sorting out the problem without involving others
   – confronting the person who is causing the problem
   – referring the problem to a higher authority, often the line manager

Key Terms	team	a group of people working together in order to achieve defined objectives
	effective	achieving the objectives that have been set
	grievance procedure	the formal procedure to follow when you have a complaint against your employer

Activities

7.1 Write down five qualities a team member should ideally possess to enable the team to function effectively.

7.2 A new colleague, Jake, has just joined your team, and you find him to be an absolute pain – he thinks he knows everything, and doesn't. He also talks about colleagues and the line manager behind their backs.

What action could you take to deal with a character like Jake?

7.3 You have been asked by your line manager at 9.30 in the morning to carry out an urgent task for him by lunchtime. You realise that you will not be able to do this if you also finish off some figures required by the senior Finance Manager by 11.30.

Select the most appropriate action to take from the list shown below.

✔

Stop everything that you are doing at the moment and carry out the task required by your line manager.	
Email the senior Finance Manager and tell her that you will not be able to provide the figures by 11.30 because your line manager has asked you to do an urgent task.	
Ask one of your colleagues who owes you a favour to do the urgent task for you.	
Explain to your line manager that you have an 11.30 deadline for work given you by the senior Finance Manager and ask if the deadline the line manager has set can be extended or the task given to a colleague.	

7.4   Identify from the list below **three** characteristics of an effective team.

	✔
Members compete to finish their tasks as quickly as possible.	
Members understand their role in the team and what they have to do.	
Members are prepared to carry out tasks for other members if necessary.	
Members must all be professionally qualified to the same level.	
Members must maintain good levels of communication with each other.	
Members must immediately report any forms of dissatisfaction to the line manager.	

7.5   You work as an assistant in an Accounts Department. A new assistant who has recently been transferred from another section has been given a desk next to you. He spends a lot of work time chatting on his mobile phone and so is not completing his purchase invoicing work on time, and when he does complete it he sometimes makes mistakes. The Department is not very busy at the moment.

(a)   What effect could this behaviour have? Select the appropriate option.

	✔
No effect because the Department is not busy at the moment.	
It could just reflect badly on him because of his behaviour.	
It could reflect badly on the Department and also the organisation because suppliers may not get paid on time.	

(b)   What steps could you take to resolve the problem? Select the appropriate option.

	✔
Do nothing at all because you can help him and check his work.	
Mention the problem to your line manager if the situation does not improve.	
Mention the problem to the Finance Director.	

8 CPD – developing skills and knowledge at work

this chapter covers...

This chapter explains the need for an individual working in an organisation to acquire knowledge and develop a variety of skills in order to:

- *improve himself or herself*
- *meet the needs of the organisation*

A way of achieving this is to undertake a programme of Continuing Professional Development (CPD).

- *This process, which should be formally recorded by the employee, might involve:*
  - *in-house training courses and technical updates*
  - *work-shadowing*
  - *use of a work mentor*
  - *external training courses*
  - *researching the area of work on the internet and in publications*
- *Employees should be able to identify their development needs and objectives for achievement, involving their line manager in the process.*
- *These objectives should be SMART, ie **S**pecific, **M**easurable, **A**chievable, **R**ealistic and **T**ime bound.*
- *The employee should monitor and review his or her progress against these objectives on a regular basis.*
- *The development of employee skills and knowledge helps to improve the efficiency of the organisation and will benefit all concerned.*

CONTINUING PROFESSIONAL DEVELOPMENT (CPD)

what is CPD?

Continuing Professional Development (CPD) can be defined as:

the learning activities undertaken by employees to maintain, improve and broaden the knowledge and skills required in their professional lives.

Continuing Professional Development (CPD) is an ongoing cycle – a process involving both employee and employer. It is normally up to the employee to complete the planned activities in order to achieve the level of professional competence required by the professional body to which he or she belongs.

Whether you are currently working in accounting or not, your studies require you to be aware of the processes and benefits of CPD. For the purposes of this chapter, you should assume that you or the person described are working in an accounting department.

Study the diagram below and then read the text that follows.

start here

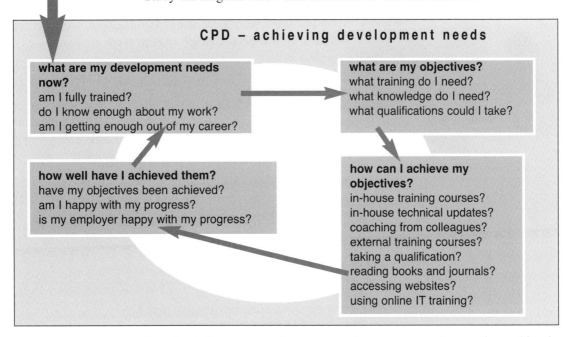

CPD – achieving development needs

what are my development needs now?
am I fully trained?
do I know enough about my work?
am I getting enough out of my career?

what are my objectives?
what training do I need?
what knowledge do I need?
what qualifications could I take?

how well have I achieved them?
have my objectives been achieved?
am I happy with my progress?
is my employer happy with my progress?

how can I achieve my objectives?
in-house training courses?
in-house technical updates?
coaching from colleagues?
external training courses?
taking a qualification?
reading books and journals?
accessing websites?
using online IT training?

In order to improve **performance** and career prospects, people working in accounting need to take stock of their current position and identify exactly where it is they want to go. The diagram above shows a process which involves four stages:

1   what are my development needs now?

2   what are my objectives?

3 how can I achieve my objectives?

4 how well have I achieved them?

The process is continuous and subject to continual review. We will look at each of the four stages in turn.

WHAT ARE MY DEVELOPMENT NEEDS NOW?

You will first need to carry out a form of personal 'audit' of your **knowledge** (what you know) and **skills** (how you put it into practice). How do you do this? You need to ask yourself a number of questions and also talk them over with colleagues:

1 Am I content with what I am doing at present?

2 Am I confident that I have the background knowledge for my work?

3 Am I up-to-date with changes in the knowledge and skills required for the area in which I work ?

talk it over with your manager

4 Do I need further training for what I am doing at work?

5 Do my skills need developing? For example, do I need to go on a spreadsheet course? Do I need to improve my computer skills?

6 Where do I see myself working in a year's time?

If you are at work you may well discuss these issues on a regular basis with your manager as part of the **appraisal** process. At the interview, objectives should be set, training needs identified and promotion prospects explored.

You should always be given the opportunity of discussing with your manager the ways in which you can develop your **skills** and **knowledge** and improve your performance.

WHAT ARE MY OBJECTIVES?

When you have thought about your development and career needs, and discussed them with others, you will be in a position to set specific objectives – targets – for achievement. These will not be vague and woolly like 'I want to be a manager' or 'I want to be better at my work' but will be very specific. For example you might say that within the next twelve months . . . .

'I need to learn more about spreadsheets because they are used a lot in the Accounts Department.'

'I need to learn more about the Sage computer accounting system. I can do the basics, but haven't a clue about doing journal entries.'

'I'd like to do an accounting qualification – it should help me to get on in my career.'

'I need to know more about the theoretical background to the accounting work I am doing at the moment.'

These objectives may be met through a variety of activities, for example:

- **on-the-job training** – being coached by another employee, work-shadowing, attending formal in-house courses, following 'tutorials' provided online or with software used in the office

- **technical updates** carried out in-house – for example, using updated payroll software at the beginning of a new tax year, or when a new software version is released, and making use of the technical telephone 'helpline' offered by the software company (eg by Sage)

- **external training courses** run by your organisation (if it has a separate training centre) or by an independent training body – for example a Health & Safety course or Excel spreadsheet course run by the local Chamber of Commerce or College

- **research** on the internet or through reading publications related to the tasks you do at work – for example, if you work in an Accounts Department you may need to get up-to-date with the ever-increasing internal security measures needed for handling debit and credit card transactions

- taking **qualifications** such as a Level 2 qualification in Accounting and Finance – studying at a local college or with a distance learning provider

The important point here is that you cannot expect to do everything at once. You should have the opportunity to sit down with your manager and work out a suitable and realistic programme which can be followed and then reviewed after a set period of time.

objectives that are SMART

When setting objectives you should always aim for **SMART** objectives. SMART is a widely used acronym which, when used in CPD, helps to ensure that the objectives set are suitable and effective for the person concerned. In practice, the words represented by these letters do vary to a certain extent, but a common example requires that the objectives should be:

Specific

Measurable

Achievable

Realistic

Time bound

In other words, each of the CPD objectives agreed with the employee's manager should be:

- **Specific** – they should be clear and well-defined so that the employee knows what is expected and the manager can monitor and assess how successful the employee is at achieving each objective.

- **Measurable** – the employee and the manager should be able to tell how well the objective is being achieved. For example if the employee is taking an external course or qualification, there will be exam success rates to provide a measure of success.

- **Achievable** – the objective must be within the competence of the employee. All resources needed by the employee must be made available by the management (eg equipment, time, access to people, funding for an external course).

- **Realistic** – this relates in a way to 'achievable' and asks whether the employee is able and willing to work to achieve the target set. In short, does the employee have the necessary 'belief'?

- **Time bound** – a timescale must be set for the objective. Can the objective be achieved within the time target?

PLANNING – HOW CAN I ACHIEVE MY OBJECTIVES?

The SMART objectives the employee plans to achieve by definition need to be made very specific. For example:

'I need to go on an advanced Excel spreadsheet course at the local Chamber of Commerce Training Centre so that I can process the sales data and produce charts for my manager.'

'I need to work alongside Kulvinder for a week so that I can learn more about operating our Sage computer accounting system.'

'I want to enrol on a Level 2 course in accounting at the local college because I want to be promoted within the department.'

'I need to read that Osborne Books accounting textbook recommended by my colleague because it will give me the background knowledge I need.'

You may already have identified the fact that what this person really needs to do is to enrol on an accounting course with a training provider. This will provide the theoretical and practical background to a career in an accounts office and also help with promotion prospects, as will be seen in the Case Study at the bottom of this page.

HOW WELL HAVE I ACHIEVED? AND WHAT NEXT?

The process of personal planning never stands still. As in any planning process, achievement will have to be monitored on a regular basis, eg every twelve months, at the annual appraisal interview when both the employer and the employee will need to re-assess the situation. The planning process can then start all over again – new objectives, new targets, a new action plan.

In the Case Study which follows we look at the personal planning carried out by a typical accounting employee.

Case Study

CPD – MAKING THE MOST OF YOUR RESOURCES

situation

Kelly works in the Accounts Department of CompLink Limited, a computer supplies wholesaler. She moves to some extent between the sections, but spends most of her time in Sales Ledger, where she processes orders on the computer accounting system, checks documentation and has started basic work in Credit Control, sending out statements.

Kelly wants to get on in her job and career. At her appraisal interview in July, she agreed with her manager that she should achieve certain targets within the next twelve months as part of her Continuing Professional Development.

These objectives included:

- in-house training in credit control procedures in the Accounts Department, achieved by work-shadowing (working alongside a senior colleague in Credit Control)

- attending an intensive two day training course in computer accounting at a local external training provider

- enrolment at the local college to take a Level 2 Accounting course, which runs from September to the following June

solution

Kelly makes good use of the various resources chosen to help her in her CPD:

colleagues

Kelly can talk to her colleagues and make the most of their experience and knowledge, picking up tips about dealing with procedures and situations. This is particularly useful in Credit Control where Kelly can learn how to deal with slow payers - interpreting all their lame excuses about not paying (eg 'payment has been authorised but has not yet been put through the system' or 'we don't seem to have received the invoice'). She will also learn how to send out the appropriate chaser letters without offending the 'important' customers who sometimes pay late.

training provider

Studying accounting is never an easy option, but Kelly finds that having a good teacher and a lively class helps her understand the more difficult areas of the course. She is able to ask questions about the areas she finds difficult and is given help when her trial balance doesn't balance.

textbooks

Kelly uses the Osborne Books range of accounting texts and finds that they help her understand difficult concepts and prepare well for her assessments. She is online at home and finds the resources on the publisher's website (www.osbornebooks.co.uk) a big help. She has also invested in the Osborne Books pocket-sized 'Wise Guides' which are very handy for revision.

other websites

The websites of accounting bodies such as AAT are full of useful information and links. The site www.aat.org.uk provides Student Forums and offers e-learning opportunities.

Kelly also uses the website of HM Revenue & Customs (www.HMRC.gov.uk) to answer queries about VAT which have cropped up at work.

and finally . . .

At the end of the twelve months Kelly will discuss with her manager the extent to which she has been successful in achieving her objectives:

- Following her in-house training and work-shadowing, is she now able to operate the customer debt chasing system without supervision?

- Did she complete her computer accounting course successfully and has she been able to take on more advanced input work?

- Did she pass her accounting exams?

She will then be in a position to set the objectives for the following twelve months. For example she may have further in-house training, go on a computer spreadsheet course, and take the next stage of her accounting qualification.

RECORDING CPD

It is important to record CPD as an ongoing process so that the employee and employer can monitor and review its success or shortcomings, and take appropriate action as necessary.

There is no set format for a CPD record, but a typical form will include sections to cover the overall **goal** of CPD as discussed with the manager, and the specific objectives – **learning needs –** which will enable the goal to be achieved. The record should be kept up-to-date and form the basis of a regular (eg six-monthly) discussion between employer and employee.

The extract from a sample AAT CPD form shown on the next page includes:

- details of the employee and job title
- a description of the main responsibilities of the employee
- a table set out in four columns detailing the CPD process:

Assess ➤ Plan ➤ Action ➤ Evaluate

These four columns require the following details:

Assess column involves an assessment of what the employee needs in the way of training and study, specifically:

– CPD goals

– learning needs

– training gaps

Plan column

– what are the activities involved in the learning and study process

– the target dates?

Action column

– what progress have you made with the activities in the previous column?

– have you completed the activities, yes or no?

Evaluate column

– Learning Outcomes – what have you learnt from the activities?

– Reflection – your personal comments on what you have achieved, ie was it what you had planned, or do you need further activities to achieve these goals?

And last but not least - what comes next? The CPD process now starts all over again for the next stage of personal development, identifying needs, setting objectives, monitoring progress and further evaluation.

AAT CPD record   **Name:**   **AAT no:**   **Dates:**

Your job title: Assistant Accountant in the Finance Department of a construction company.

Your main responsibilities or your MIP approved areas:

My role involves dealing with various areas, including: purchase ledger, sales ledger, payroll, month end procedures. My manager has recently asked me to take on some new challenges. These include helping to prepare monthly management accounts and co-ordinating the work of a new member of staff. I enjoy my current role and look forward to getting involved in these new tasks. I'd like to develop my role further and move into a management position in the future.

Assess	Plan	Action	Evaluate	
CPD goals/learning needs/training gaps	**Activities**	**Done?**	**Learning outcomes**	**Reflection**
What do you need to learn to achieve your career goals? What are your learning needs/training gaps? What do you already do well and where could you improve? *For example, learn about payroll year end procedures or develop project management skills.*	*What learning activities will help you to meet your needs?* *For example, job shadowing my manager, attending a course or listening to a podcast.*	*What is the progress of your learning? Have you completed the planned activities?*	*What have you learned as a result of each activity?*	*How useful has the learning been? Have you achieved the goals you set yourself? How did or will this impact on your work?*
Payroll: Identify and understand implications of relevant income tax and NIC changes.	Activity: Read HMRC Employer Bulletin. Also check HMRC news on Twitter.	Yes No	Updated knowledge about the company van usage rules. Need more information about the CIS changes.	Very informative but I think I'll need more detailed info on the new CIS scheme – hence a new learning need will be added to my 2012/2013 CPD record.
Purchase ledger and Sales ledger: My goals is to continue to maintain purchase and sales ledger accurately and efficiently. As my knowledge and skills in these areas are up to date, I don't have any learning needs at the moment. Will reassess in the next CPD cycle.	Activity:	Yes No		

sample CPD form, courtesy of the AAT

Chapter Summary

- Improving performance through Continuing Professional Development (CPD) involves a number of stages, starting with an assessment of current knowledge and skills and the need for further training and study.

- Defined objectives and associated activities can be planned and defined – often in an appraisal interview.

- These objectives should be 'SMART':
    Specific
    Measurable
    Achievable
    Realistic
    Time bound

- An employee should then work out how he or she is going to achieve these objectives, assessing the resources that are going to be needed. These could include tapping into the expertise of colleagues, training in-house, taking a qualification, obtaining study material in various media.

- The final stage in the personal development process is to review and evaluate progress and to establish new targets and action plans. This may be carried out with the employer as part of the regular appraisal process.

- All stages in the CPD process should be clearly documented.

Key Terms

CPD	Continuing Professional Development (CPD) involves an agreed set of learning activities undertaken by employees to maintain, improve and broaden the knowledge and skills required in their professional lives
objectives	specific 'SMART' targets for development needs
knowledge	what an employee needs to know to be able to work effectively
skills	the ability to put knowledge into practice
appraisal	the process whereby a manager interviews an employee on a regular basis, assessing past performance and identifying development needs
performance	the success rate in achieving development needs

Activities

8.1 The four stages in the CPD process are set out below on the left. You are to match them with the four statements which are set out on the right. Draw lines linking the appropriate statements with the four stages.

Stages

Identifying needs

Setting objectives

Planning and achieving objectives

Evaluation

Statements

Passed the AAT Level 2 exams

Examining weaknesses in knowledge and skills

Deciding to go on a spreadsheet course

Discussing achievement of objectives with the line manager

8.2 'SMART' when describing objectives stands for:

Specific	
Measurable	
Achievable	
Realistic	
Time bound	

Write in the table against each of the SMART objectives the appropriate sentence from the following options which relate to a student considering studying for a qualification at evening classes.

'It needs to be completed by June.'

'It needs to be well defined.'

'I know I can do it if I work really hard.'

'My employer is financing my studies.'

'My exam results will be a test of my success.'

8.3 Who are the main people who are involved in CPD discussions and what should they be able to achieve in their discussions during the course of the CPD?

Answers to activities

CHAPTER 1: ACCOUNTING AND FINANCE IN THE WORKPLACE

1.1 (a)

1.2 (b)

1.3 (a)

1.4 (c)

1.5 Internal auditors are employees of the organisation (or people contracted in from outside) to look over its accounting systems; external auditors are independent firms who are contracted by the shareholders of larger companies to validate the accounts.

1.6 (a) – sales ledger assistant to accounts line manager

– cashier to accounts line manager

– payroll assistant to accounts line manager

(b) the sales ledger assistant

(c) the cashier in the first place, the line manager in the second place

(d) purchases ledger, costing, inventory control

CHAPTER 2: EFFICIENCY AND REGULATION IN THE WORKPLACE

2.1 (b)

2.2 (c)

2.3 (b)

2.4 (d)

2.5 (b)

2.6 (d)

2.7 (a)

CHAPTER 3: ETHICAL BEHAVIOUR AND SUSTAINABILITY

3.1   Objectivity, Equality, Professional competence and due care.

3.2   You mention to a member of your family that a shop in the High Street that is one of your customers is having financial problems and is likely to become insolvent.

3.3

You mention to your partner that her employer has been refused credit by the company that employs you.	**confidentiality**
Your line manager says that he needs another assistant, but the new employee 'must be under 20 as the pay rate will be lower'.	**equality**
You 'borrow' £10 from the cash till because you are short of cash for the weekend. You fully intend to put it back on Monday, but you forget as it is such a busy day.	**integrity**
You hear a colleague at a Friday night pub session in a crowded bar say that his manager is 'useless' and he 'doesn't know how he got his qualifications'.	**professional behaviour**

3.4   A cycle to work scheme.

A policy of re-using the blank side of A4 white copy paper for printing on.

Put up a notice telling staff to only fill the kettle with the amount of water needed when making coffee or tea.

Suggest a team is set up to do a charity walk in support of Cancer Research UK.

3.5   Computers should be turned off at the end of each working day.

Sustainability encourages an employer to pay for an employee to train for an accounting qualification.

CHAPTER 4: WORKING WITH NUMBERS

4.1

(a)

product code	description	quantity	price	unit	total	discount %	net
109BK	Box file (black)	20	4.00	each	80.00	30	56.00
					Total		56.00
					VAT @ 20%		11.20
					TOTAL		67.20

(b)

product code	description	quantity	price	unit	total	discount %	net
235RD	Biros (red)	9	5.60	box of ten	50.40	20	40.32
					Total		40.32
					VAT @ 20%		8.06
					TOTAL		48.38

(c)

product code	description	quantity	price	unit	total	discount %	net
563BL	Year planners (blue)	8	12.95	each	103.60	10	93.24
					Total		93.24
note that VAT is rounded <u>down</u> to nearest p					VAT @ 20%		18.64
					TOTAL		111.88

4.2 (a) 15% discount on an amount of £45.50 = £6.825, rounded to £6.83

(b) 20% discount on an amount of £44.99 = £8.998, rounded to £9.00

(c) 30% discount on an amount of £21.75 = £6.525, rounded to £6.53

(d) 15% discount on an amount of £390.95 = £58.6425, rounded to £58.64

(e) 30% discount on an amount of £964.55 = £289.365, rounded to £289.37

(f) 2.5% discount on an amount of £35.95 = £0.89875, rounded to £0.90

4.3 (a) £41.00 + VAT of £8.20
(b) £244.00 + VAT of £48.80
(c) £1.90 + VAT of £0.38
(d) £364.00 + VAT of £72.80
(e) £88.00 + VAT of £17.60

4.4

HYPNOS ENTERPRISES – Annual Sales				
	Forecast (benchmark) £	Actual £	Difference £	Percentage difference £
Year 1	600,000	642,000	+ 42,000	7%
Year 2	640,000	608,000	– 32,000	5%

HYPNOS ENTERPRISES – Annual Profits				
	Forecast (benchmark) £	Actual £	Difference £	Percentage difference £
Year 1	64,000	67,200	+ 3,200	5%
Year 2	65,000	63,050	– 1,950	3%

Comments could include the fact that both sales and profits were better than expected in Year 1, but worse than forecast in Year 2. Decisions will have to be made by management. It could be mentioned that action is likely to have to be taken to stop the drop in sales and profits. Students should not be expected to go further than this and should appreciate that it is the role of management to take the necessary decisions

4.5 Pie charts are excellent for showing proportions of a whole – and they are widely used for this – but they do not show relative quantities. They are therefore not very helpful in this context as they are clumsy in illustrating year-to-year trends: the eye cannot easily trace changes in sectors.

Also the pie charts do not tell you the actual divisional or total sales figures for the two years, so as a result you do not know if sales have increased or gone down.

4.6 • mean   £9.33
• median   £7.90
• mode   £11.00

The mean is the most arithmetically reliable as it takes all values into consideration.

CHAPTER 5: COMMUNICATION AT WORK

5.1 (d)

5.2

Its or It's? Study the four sentences below and tick the **two** correct options.

	✔
Its rubbish weather today.	
It's rubbish weather today.	✔
I do not like this film; it's not one of the best Bond films.	✔
I do not like this film; its not one of the best Bond films.	

5.3 'There', 'their' or 'they're'? Study the three sentences below and if you think any of them is wrong, write the correct word in the right-hand column.

Politicians are corrupt. Their all the same.	They're
The students forgot there calculators for the assessment.	their
They're are clever students who brought calculators.	There

5.4

Title page

(Executive) Summary

Introduction

Findings (Main Body)

Conclusions

Recommendations

Appendices

5.5

incorrect word	correction
239847244	239847224
Mrs	Miss
Colman	Coleman
dissappointed	disappointed
They're	There

5.6

From	j.mason@frankiesfashionware.co.uk

To l.wood@frankiesfashionware.co.uk

Subject Sales data for June **1**

Hi Laura

Please send me the quantity of St Tropez shades (code 9424) **2** sold

during the month of June **3** . We need this information to carry

out a costing exercise. I need the information, please, by 9 July **4** .

Many thanks and kind regards

Jamie

Accounts Department

CHAPTER 6: MANAGING YOUR WORK

6.1   A routine task is a task which is part of the everyday activity of the workplace. A non-routine task is an unexpected task. Examples should be given as appropriate.

6.2   Prioritisation of tasks is deciding on the order in which the tasks should be completed. This will depend on the importance and the urgency of the individual tasks.

6.3   (a)   An urgent task is a task which is required to be done by a specific deadline; an important task is a task for the completion of which an employee is given personal responsibility and which significantly affects other people.

(b)   The situation where the urgent task is relatively unimportant.

6.4   A suggested order for the list:

1   Distribute the departmental post.

2   Look at the section diary and compare with your 'To Do' list.

3   Check that details of hours worked (including overtime) have been received from all departments.

4   Send email to Marketing Department asking for monthly overtime figures to be sent through – they should have been received last Friday.

5   Process the hours of all the employees on the computer. Print out pay details and a payroll summary, including the schedule setting out the amount which will have to be paid to the Inland Revenue for income tax and National Insurance Contributions by 19th of the next month.

6   Pass the payroll printouts to your line manager for checking, and when approved, print out the payslips for distribution.

7   Prepare the BACS payroll schedule for the bank to process on Tuesday.

8   Pass the BACS payroll schedule to your line manager for checking.

9   Put a note in the diary for the Inland Revenue cheque to be prepared on 5th of next month.

10 Print out payroll statistics from the computer for your line manager – they are required for next week.

11 Draw up a notice advertising a staff trip out for next month.

6.5   (a)   You should go and turn the lights off as soon as an opportunity arises. It will not take long and will prevent the battery going flat.

(b)   This should be referred to your line manager. You are very busy, but the line manager should decide whether you should go – it may be possible for the line manager to delegate your work to someone else.

(c)   The friend should be told politely that you cannot speak during working hours. You could suggest a lunch-time meeting.

(d)   This looks like an obvious error, or even a fraud! You cannot take action yourself, but should refer the matter to your line manager to take action.

(e)   The work will have to be redone as a matter of urgency. The computer will have to be restarted and the data re-input (to the extent that it has not been saved). If there are further problems, the line manager will have to be alerted and technical assistance requested.

6.6   Carry on with your own work until you have the opportunity to refer the problem to your line manager when she is free.

6.7

Your line manager asks you for the balances of your top 20 customer accounts. She needs the information for a meeting that morning.	**urgent**
Your line manager asks you to provide information from the office for the accountants who are coming in next week to audit the accounts. You have never done this before as this is normally a senior colleague's responsibility.	**one-off 'ad hoc'**
Your colleague reminds you that it is your turn to get the milk from Tesco Express and remarks that the milk has run out.	**non-urgent**

6.8

An employee's personal record of tasks and events over a long period of time.	**diary**
A detailed plan which involves a number of people and interrelated tasks and events for a specific purpose over a period of time.	**action plan**
An annual guide which can be used to display staff holidays and external training courses.	**wall planner**
An employee's daily personal record of tasks to be done in the short term.	**'to do' list**

CHAPTER 7: WORKING AS A MEMBER OF A TEAM

7.1   A suggested five:

1   being pleasant and polite

2   being cooperative

3   listening to and respecting the opinions of others

4   asking for and providing help

5   do not backbite

7.2   The important point here is to make sure that your objection to Jake is based on issues which relate to the work itself rather than your personal reaction to him. You should:

•   Observe the ways in which the other members of the team deal with him – do they also have problems? If they do not, the problem may lie with you.

•   Talk the problem over with the other team members – do they think the same way?

•   Talk the matter over with Jake, if you feel you are able to.

If it emerges that the problems with Jake extend to the whole team and the standard of work and workplace efficiency is being affected, there may be a case for taking the matter to a higher authority.

7.3   Explain to your line manager that you have an 11.30 deadline for work given you by the senior Finance Manager and ask if the deadline the line manager has set can be extended or the task given to a colleague.

7.4   Members understand their role in the team and what they have to do.

Members are prepared to carry out tasks for other members if necessary.

Members must maintain good levels of communication with each other.

7.5   (a)   It could reflect badly on the Department and also the organisation because suppliers may not get paid on time.

(b)   Mention the problem to your line manager if the situation does not improve.

CHAPTER 8: CPD – DEVELOPING SKILLS AND KNOWLEDGE AT WORK

8.1   **Stages**   **Statements**

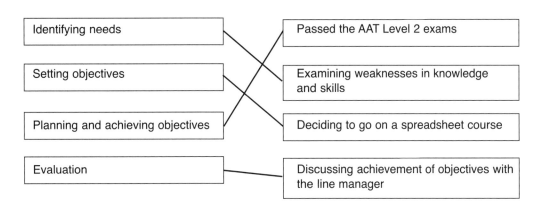

Identifying needs	Passed the AAT Level 2 exams
Setting objectives	Examining weaknesses in knowledge and skills
Planning and achieving objectives	Deciding to go on a spreadsheet course
Evaluation	Discussing achievement of objectives with the line manager

8.2   'SMART' when describing objectives stands for:

Specific	*'It needs to be well defined.'*
Measurable	*'My exam results will be a test of my success.'*
Achievable	*'My employer is financing my studies.'*
Realistic	*'I know I can do it if I work really hard.'*
Time bound	*'It needs to be completed by June.'*

8.3   The people involved are the employer and the employee. It is an important partnership for successful career progression. The result of their discussion at the planning stage of CPD should be a mutual agreement of the objectives to be set. As the objectives are set in motion, they will jointly monitor progress and be able to identify success rates and any problem areas on which they will have to take action. At the end of the CPD process they will jointly evaluate success and be able to plan the next stage in the CPD process.

Index

for your notes

for your notes

for your notes